RUNNING A FOOD TRUCK BUSINESS

A COMPLETE GUIDE FOR BEGINNERS
ABOUT HOW TO START A SUCCESSFUL FOOD TRUCK
BUSINESS, USE THE BEST MANAGEMENT TECHNIQUES, AND
INCREASE YOUR PROFIT

TONY BYRDE

Table of Contents

Introduction

The successful establishments of food trucks have been a boom in the culinary industry. They are trendy among people, and they have invaded almost every corner of every city and town. They have gained popularity primarily because they are the cheapest and simplest ways to start a business. The food truck owners do not need a fancy store, and they can begin serving their food from their corner in the streets.

Even though food trucks can grab the attention of the masses, multiple obstacles are standing in their way to build a successful business. The food truck industry is complicated. The business model of food trucks has to be followed to reach success. Otherwise, the food owners will fail to become a successful player in the industry.

"If you plan on owning and operating your food truck, you should expect long workdays. A food truck operator's daily routine is long and tedious: planning, shopping, prepping, marketing, cooking, selling, cleaning, storing, bookkeeping, forecasting, scheduling, advertising, etc. You will soon become an expert on many restaurant business domains, adding to this the joys of mechanical issues of your trucks and weather hazards.

Start with your business plan. Grab your favorite pen and a paper pad, and start writing down all your ideas to establish a business model and a brand. Financial planning is key, and beyond the construction and build-out costs, you will need an operating budget to cover the first difficult months on the road. Networking and consulting is critical as it will help avoid errors that would be inevitable if you were launching yourself in the adventure with no consul.

It's essential to know the local and regional regulations, including permit and certification needed to get your business started. Education is key as the foodservice industry, as rewarding as it seems, is extremely detailed and exhaustive. Food truck operators are responsible for the happiness of their customers and their safety. Research is crucial, on the legislative side of the business, but also the operational aspect of the mobile food venture." (National Food Truck Association)

With a plethora of information available today, it cannot be easy to know which one works. But there's no need for you to worry. Allow this book to be your ultimate guide on running a food truck business. Thanks to this book, you can turn your passion into a full-time income! So, what are you waiting for? There's no time to waste. Start to read!

Chapter 1. Twenty Good Reasons to Start a Food Truck Business

From Los Angeles to New York, street food is everywhere. Since 2009 the food truck business has befitted 80%. According to Statista, *"In 2015, the value of the U.S. food truck industry increased to 856.7 million U.S. dollars. The industry was forecasted to increase by another 140 million U.S. dollars by 2020."* IBISWorld also states that: *"The Food Trucks industry has expanded over the five years to 2019 and is one of the best-performing segments in the broader foodservice sector. The industry's remarkable rise is largely attributable to changing*

consumer preferences in favor of unique, gourmet cuisine at less expensive prices." Well, in last years, food trucks are setting deep roots, and here are twenty reasons why this trend is so hot.

1. Changing Perceptions

Away are the days when mobile kitchens were classified as "Roach Coaches." People understand street food businesses are held to the same (in some cases, higher) sanitation and safety standards as any café.

2. Value

Lunch wagons give an economical meal for the frugal foodie. Generally, street food is more affordable than conventional feasting alternatives.

3. Lower Overhead

Portable kitchens have a more affordable working cost than physical bistros. With no rent to pay or working to help, food trucks can run a lean and compensating action less expensive than their regular eating rivals.

4. Lower Startup Cost

It can cost well over $1 million dollars to start a restaurant. You can start a mobile food business for under $75,000 in most situations.

5. Location

One of the biggest risks of starting a restaurant is that you're pretty much stuck in one place. Over time the demographics and appeal of a certain city can decline. A food truck can travel to where the most business is every day.

6. Cooperation

Lunch truck administrators are an outstandingly close association that participates, so everybody profits from one another business.

7. Marketing

A tremendous mechanical assembly is a moving board. Each time they are all over town, they are publicizing. Seeing a fiercely conditioned development van shrouded with logos in a business region makes buzz and drives deals.

8. Healthy Options

Various adaptable kitchens serve wieners and southern style treats. Anyway, many are doing veggie-dear, sans gluten, and vegan suppers to consider strong tastes. Some food trucks have dared to quite outrageous as making sound choices.

9. Social Media

Food truck operators are bosses of computerized communication, and they use it to drive deals. Their tweets, Pinterest entries, blogs, and Facebook pages are continually developing promoting platforms that people have embraced in general.

10. Fast Food

Do you need your lunch hot and lively? A food truck gives time-starved citizens a fast eat without the holding up uptime of a plunk down cabaret.

11. Choices

Purchasers like choices. A few food trucks forgot about giving hungry citizens a significantly remarkably modified menu to blend and match their victory as per their tendencies. You can enjoy an hors d'oeuvre, stroll around to another truck and get burritos, and in case you're so far greedy, take a gander at a yogurt truck.

12. Culture

Each possible ethnic, planning style and taste by food are addressed by food trucks. Buyers can eat Maine lobster on the west shore of California food on the east coast. Bistros can plunge into Korean, French, Italian, Thai, Greek,

Ethiopian, Japanese or American food. On the occasion that you're a food truck lover, anything is possible for you.

13. Fusion Flavors

Japanese tacos? Surely. German Gyros? Accelerate it. Mexican Pizza? More, if it's not all that much difficulty, creative gourmet experts are pushing the mix envelope to make fascinating, spellbinding, and delicious commitments to satisfy striking foodies.

14. The Fame Game

Spike Mendelsohn, Tom Colicchio, Jose Andres, and Jamie Oliver have run food trucks. Some eminent Chefs use flexible kitchens to test plans and thoughts for their restaurants. Food trucks enable VIP Chefs to explore different streets concerning strategies without risk and show up at a broader market. This example will proceed since people love superstars.

15. Fun Factor

Street food is an unobtrusive energy elective. Proprietors attempt to offer attractive eating up experience to their customers in the city. Workers can move away from their work area territory and experience a festival atmosphere on their dispatch daybreak. The marvelously covered mechanical assemblies are fun; the food is fun; and the people taking your solicitation are engaging.

16. The American Dream

Foodies understand that street food vendors give occupations and represent a massive organization in the metropolitan territories where they run. People are more willing to give their money to an active entrepreneur than to a mysterious association. Street food vendors additionally help deals in the retail areas where they work.

17. Fresh Air

Exactly when the atmosphere is charming, nothing is better than going outside. An exuberant walk around the redirection spot to a lunch truck is what the expert mentioned to lift eaters' spirits in the healthy wild. Who needs additional Chinese in the same workplace where you work 8-10 daily?

18. Novelty

Food trucks offer a novel approach to eating out from the developing menu alternatives to new units on the scene. Mobile cooking gives a fascinating eating niche to customers who have become tired of being continually blasted by messages from chain cafés and corporate fast food.

19. Fresh and Local

Mobile kitchens are bringing the farm-to-table idea to urban communities over the world. Chefs purchase proteins, dairy, and produce from neighborhood sources and create food fresher and tastier than that offered in brick and mortar restaurants. Customers can feel the distinction between those small scale greens grown down the road compared to the salad processed in a factory several miles away.

20.Street Food Tastes Good

Regardless of whether it's escargot or burger, road Chefs are making beautiful suppers. The assortment, quality, and deliciousness of mobile food are faltering and embraced by the world. From delectable, upscale meals to artery-clogging deep-fried, street food tastes excellent, and therefore, food trucks are here to stay.

Chapter 2. How to Start This Business

We did the research and put you in the sweat equity. Since no small business owner would leap into a blind $1.2 billion market, we're putting together a convenient reference guide, so you know exactly what to expect.

Because food trucks are micro-restaurants on wheels, you may expect that starting up a food truck company would cost you just a fraction of that of a conventional full-service, brick-and-mortar restaurant. You are right, to a certain extent. But that doesn't mean it will be a comfortable ride down Main Street in your new set of shiny wheels for lunch hour. Costs will vary when starting a mobile operation (just like for any restaurant), but you can assume to pay between $28,000 and $114,000. It can depend on many factors. Below is a couple to consider.

Write a Business Plan

First of all, the food truck industry is highly competitive. What started as a gold rush has evolved into a more mature market for ambitious entrepreneurs. Experienced restaurateurs flock to space to get their pie slices and also use food trucks as a tool to advertise their main restaurants.

You will need to do a large amount of preparation to maximize the chance of winning against this degree of competition. Understanding your market and the unique value you deliver, as well as the nuts and bolts of financing, insuring, and licensing your transaction, is essential. Working out a traditional business plan is the best way to do that.

If you do it yourself, your time is the main cost, but if this is your first business scheme, you should pay an expert to transcribe the plan and refer to any legal and tax requirements you will have to meet. The cost here can range from a few hundred to several thousand dollars, depending on your operation's sophistication and the amount of work you need to do.

Things You Need to Purchase

The actual truck is the most apparent startup cost for a food truck business. But irrespective of that, the cost of buying your truck needs to be addressed. Prices can differ as they do for other cars. You will come across a brand spanking new food truck, Lamborghini, as well as your 1985 Jalopy Garden. The price of a food truck will take you anywhere from $50,000 to $200,000, depending on whether you're going down the brand new or used one. This also doesn't include the expense of decorating and equipping the truck—such as designing and installing a truck cover, as well as accumulating any other stoves, fryers, or freezers you may need to cook your specialty food. But if you're uncertain about dropping $200K on a truck, we suggest hitting the bottom end and then equipping it as required.

Ultimately, bear in mind that bigger may not always be better. Not only does a giant truck usually costs more, but if yours weighs more than 26,000 pounds, you'll need a commercial driver's license even to drive it. It can cost anything between $100-$300 for state licensing and up to $1000-$3000 if you're going to toss in the extra expense of commercial driver's lessons to make sure you're qualified to pass a CDL road test.

Food and Other Supplies

You will also need to invest some of your startup money in buying the food and equipment you need to produce and serve your food. Restaurant experts say that your food cost should be 28%-35% of the price you sell the commodity. So, if you're selling a taco for

18

$1.00, your food cost for that taco should be $0.28-$0.35; otherwise, you'll risk going into cash flow problems in the future.

Insurance for the Food Truck (and Business)

You heard right, just as with any small (or big) business you have to insure. Expected insurance costs to get your food truck going could be about $300, increasing annually. You must ensure your food truck is insured for anything: general liability insurance, automobile accidents, foodborne disease, workers' compensation for you and your employees.

Licenses, Permits, and Certifications

We cannot talk about how much it costs to start a food truck without thinking about the licenses, permits, and certifications you will need to run your food truck business. You'll have to jump through a few hoops in addition to the health department to get the right permits, so you'll still have to pay to apply for them. These products should be factored in as part of your startup costs and maintenance costs when planning your business strategy for food trucks, depending on how much you need to renew.

It is a tricky problem as the laws, regulations, and costs vary from one state to another and from one town or county to another. The best counsel we can give you here is to check all local (state, city, county, district, township, etc...) jurisdictions once you know what corner of the street you want to operate to get the proper licensing.

On the other hand, many of these rules, legislation, and ordinances are becoming more relaxed due to food truck vendors' popularity. Make it simpler in your town for food truck vendors.

Gas for the Truck

Another recurring cost to consider is that of gas. Like many of your startup costs for food trucks, the fuel cost will vary depending on your truck's size, how much you drive, where you fill up, and any additional equipment you may be used as generators. Expect to spend between $250 and $500 monthly to preserve your wheels turning and the incomes coming.

POS System

Fast-moving lines are equal to content clients, whereas content clients are equal to repeat business. Food trucks were cash-only businesses back in the day. This is no longer the case, so taking card payments is ideal. As mobile payments grow in popularity, people are gradually beginning to bring less and less cash out with them. With the growing cashless phenomenon, food trucks understand that accepting cards and mobile payments can increase their income dramatically. But to do so, you'll need to invest in a POS system.

While the expense of a cloud-based retail location framework may differ, there is a sensibly evaluated framework with dependable help for about $1,000 or less.

Promoting Your Food Truck Business

Your promoting should be on its game with the measure of competition you'll be confronting. This implies zeroing in on a substantial web-based media presence and elegant email lobbies for a few food trucks.

The food business is exceptionally visual, seems excellent and ideal to be promoted on a site like Instagram. Taking and posting exquisite photographs of your food should be your need, yet you can do much more than that. Hotshot your vehicles' marking, take pictures of clients gathering around your car, and even offer some photographs in the background. For instance, Instagram's Stories highlight is an ideal method to show the different stages of setting up a supper.

As you will probably leave your food truck at different spots during the day, you may likewise need to share this sort of information continuously. Twitter and Facebook are fantastic devices to make such a moment update conceivable. They're similarly fundamental gadgets to send your fans broader updates. For instance, you can make a Facebook occasion and welcome your fans to join if you will be at a food truck swarm/celebration a long way ahead in the month.

Finally, you would prefer not to belittle the impact of email advertising. There is no better method to interface with a client than employing email on a 1:1 premise. "POS frameworks, for example, "shopkeep," make making your email list straightforward

21

when ringing up an exchange. You would then give those clients restrictive arrangements to get them back for future discussions and general messages with data.

While showcasing is both pragmatic and fundamental, it's not modest. When you follow our rules, here are the costs you should be considering:

- Your time to deal with the promoting channels or low maintenance employ: $10-$25 60 minutes

- Custom email formats: $100+

- Subscription to the email promoting stage: $10-$200+ a month

One significant bit of information is that some email advertising stages offer a free form of their product, which you can use when you're merely firing up, and your rundown is little. Most will likewise incorporate free layouts for the plan to assist you with the beginning.

Hiring and Training Employees

We know that when you throw open the windows to your brand-new vehicle, recruiting staff may not be the first object on your mind, but that's certainly something you need to keep in mind and prepare for accordingly. Ideally, you want your business to expand and prosper. All that sounds like is longer lines, more orders, and higher sales. The duration of your lunch hour line may double suddenly, so you'll need help (i.e., a paying employee) to help you take orders and stack the tacos and ring up sales.

You may want to start with more than one employee, based on your truck's size and the length of your line. You should also consider staff with prior experience with food trucks or restaurants. It will help speed up the learning curve and provide the quality service your customers would enjoy. Furthermore, irrespective of the workforce's size, it is expected that each employee will be paid between $8 and $15 an hour.

Besides the time and expense of locating and recruiting employees, you should include some extra costs. For example, if you want your workers to wear attires—whether it's a basic t-shirt or apron, or somewhat more intricate—you'll have to buy those. Your workers might also need to receive food safety training and even obtain a qualification for food handling, depending on your state.

The costs associated with such items can vary considerably, depending on how you choose to run your business, as well as the state in which you work.

Put Money Back in Your Pocket

Now we want to leave you with a way of putting some money back in your wallet. Because there are many costs involved in opening a mobile food truck business, it's also a chance for you to turn the tables around and earn a few dollars promotion.

That's right, and you should carve out a small portion of real estate on your truck to use as advertising space, as the truck owner. Find another local business that would complement yours, or one which is also important to your demographic goals and sell some room for publicity. For something that works with all parties, you will discuss the rate and the term.

Such food truck startup costs are by no means everything you'll need to invest in when you start your food truck company. Nonetheless, they are a couple of the more expensive elements to consider when deciding how much it would cost to launch your food truck.

Chapter 3. Kinds of Mobile Food Vehicles

P icking the correct truck is seemingly the main purchasing choice you'll make when beginning a food truck business. We diagram the key contemplations you'll have to remember when making this buy and give some famous alternatives.

Food Trucks

Food trucks favor most merchants in the portable food industry in light of their reach in sizes and their versatility. They offer space and room for flexibility. The average food trucks usually range anywhere from 14 to 34 feet in length. The large space gives you room to cook your meals there and serve them. By definition, a food truck is an authorized, portable mechanized vehicle or unit which is used for offering prepared food alternatives to the overall population. This definition is very dubious. However, that might be because the meaning of a food truck changes from city to city.

Food Carts

Food carts are unique concerning food trucks in that they don't go under their capacity. These trucks are towed by a vehicle and are ordinarily dropped off for the time they're allowed, at times, several years. Food trailers combine features of both the food truck and food cart. Similarly, a trailer has plenty of room like a food truck. It will most likely have a good-sized kitchen and plenty of

26

space for storage. A trailer allows you to serve a large crowd and keep cooking.

Food Trailers

Much like food trucks, food trailers come up short on a drivetrain framework and in this way require a vehicle to tow them to the areas where merchants intend to sell their admission. Often beginners decide to start with a food cart, as they are small with low maintenance. They are quite simple and you can attach them to your car and tow them to your designated area. When you choose a food cart, you should be okay with having a small working area, if not, this isn't the vehicle for you. Additionally, if you want to serve large amounts of food at once, that won't be possible with a food cart.

Bustaurant – an Eatery Inside a Transport

So far, in the versatile food industry set of practices, eating at food trucks in numerous areas of the nation is an interesting eating experience. In any case, cafes in the Los Angeles, California, or Sarasota Springs, New York, zones need to feast someplace that exemplifies something remarkable. Cafes in these two urban communities currently have another versatile food alternative: the bustaurant, a café inside a transport.

Rather than the regular remaining at a check, requesting, and eating, the clients of these new diners are given the alternative to step installed and be situated at tables inside the transport. Even though these transports are equipped with best in class kitchens, the laws direct them to forbid kitchen activity while they're moving.

Hence, a large portion of the food is set up off-site or in the kitchen just while the transport is halted in an assigned stopping zone.

Ford Stepvan (UPS truck)

You have presumably observed a great deal of these sorts of vans in your neighborhood, particularly if you live in the US.

These are ordinarily used for business exercises by bundle conveyance organizations, for example, UPS and Fed-Ex.

The 1971 models are mainstream for food truck changes as they are roomy.

Pony Boxes

As the name proposes, horsebox trailers were used to move ponies and are presently being changed over into all kinds of versatile providing food units.

They are regularly changed over into portable espresso or liquor bars and are exceptionally famous at weddings and private occasions.

Citroen H Vans

Citroen H vans are old French board vans which were underway somewhere in the range of 1941 and 1981.

They have gotten extremely famous in the most recent ten years or thereabouts, particularly in the UK. They have a vintage look and appeal to them and are unquestionably eye acting when they have been changed over into a food truck.

Caravans

Vintage or retro caravans are another mainstream kind of vehicle being changed over and utilized as food trucks.

They are moderately small-sized, making them simple to tow and store, contrasted with some different sorts of vehicles used for food trucks. Vintage caravans are to purchase second hand.

School Transports

American style school transports are presently beginning to spring up in the food truck scene.

The yellow bodywork makes such a truck very eyecatching, and they likewise offer a great deal of room when changed over for preparing, and serving food.

Piaggio Ape

The Piaggio Ape is a 3-wheeled light business bike created by an Italian organization and has been in nonstop creation since 1948. Its reduced size assists with exploring Italy's tight roads and are likewise used as spring upmarket slows down.

They are a famous decision for changing over to sell items that needn't bother with a lot of room to prepare and create, for example, espresso and sandwiches.

This is because they are exceptionally tiny, in contrast with most other food truck transformations out there.

Airstreams

These famous American trailers have been created since the 1930s by an American organization and were initially used as movement trailers. Be that as it may, similar to a ton of interesting looking vehicles, airstream trailers are additionally being changed over into food trucks and food trailers.

VW Beetle

This notorious VW transport, authoritatively known as Volkswagen type 2 and manufactured by VW (Volkswagen) during the 1950s, was initially made for outdoors and light business use.

Presently, they are a mainstream vehicle for the road food enthusiast and changed over into creations as versatile bars and coffeehouses.

Planes

The image above is of an old DC-3 WW2 airplane changed over into a food truck, which is arranged at Aeronautical Museum in Compton, California.

Peugeot J9

This kind of van was created by Peugeot in French and Turkey for around ten years, somewhere in the lapse during 1981 and 1991.

I haven't seen a significant number of these sorts of vans around on the food truck scene; however, the ones I have, stick out. What's more, along these lines, it settles on the Peugeot J9 an extraordinary decision for a food truck.

Shipping Containers

They are used to move products all around the globe. They do not actually represent a vehicle but rather, to a greater extent, a versatile unit. People are discovering all sorts of employments for containers, from homes to office use.

They are also being changed over into portable food units by being welded onto trucks' rear (see picture). They are likewise being used as a fixed area café.

Tuk Taxi

Tuk Tuks, otherwise called auto cart, is a taxi that takes individuals all around clamoring urban areas in South-East Asia.

If you have ever been to Thailand or India, you would have certainly seen or ridden in one of these.

Starting in 2019, Bajaj Auto of Pune in India is the biggest maker of tuk-tuks on the planet.

Chapter 4. How to Get the Vehicle

The investment capital necessary to open a food truck varies depending on different cases: are you going to borrow money? Are you buying a car or a trailer? Do you need a vehicle to pull the trailer? Is the food truck already set up?

Prices can vary drastically depending on the city you're living in and the time of year. Owners usually sell at the end of the high season. You can find many offers on the market and less demand because buyers will not be able to use the food truck before the following season. Even if you won't use your food truck straight away, it is a good time to buy as you can negotiate very low prices! In our experience in WA, prices to start a food truck vary from $15000 to $100000. If you find a good pact and you are resourceful, it is quite easy to get everything ready to go for less than $20000. However, if you want a tailor-made food truck delivered to your place, you can multiply this price by five at least!

Find the Money to Get Started

To get the money you need, here are a few ideas:

- **Crowdfunding:** There are crowdfunding websites on which you can share your project and attract investors from all around the world. We're thinking about Kickstarter, Fund Me, Indiegogo, and many more. Most of those platforms take a percentage of the amount of money you gather and run for a limited time. Your project will need to be consistent and interesting so that strangers decide to invest their money in it. You also need to offer «rewards» to people who donate money on Kickstarter, for example. PayPal also recently launched their crowdfunding platform, which is supposed to be with no fees. Find more information about these platforms and select the one that will suit you the most!

- **Get a loan:** Another option is to get a loan from your bank. You will need a solid business plan to present to your banker to get this loan approved. It is unfortunately very difficult to obtain loans in Australia for buying a food truck. We saw a few people's requests for a loan being rejected for a food truck. Banks seem to be a bit reluctant to see the instability of the market and the activity's unstable nature.

- **Family and associates:** You can also inquire your family or friends to invest in your food truck if they are willing to help.

- **Our experience:** After having worked for a while in Australia, we had the necessary savings to fund our project by ourselves, without having to look for an external source of financing. The two of us had $20000 to spend on the project. If you have already worked in Australia, you know that even the most basic jobs are well paid. For example, we used to work on a construction site to clean up (paid $25 an hour) we could get between $700 and $1000 per week after tax depending on the number of hours we worked (40 to 60 hours). If you work as a waiter in a restaurant, you can also get $20 to $25 an hour. If you are willing to do many hours, you could save money quite quickly! This depends once again on which city you're living in because wages and cost of living are not the same everywhere. If you are a group of people participating in the project, if you have a good salary and know how to control your spending, you could collect the money necessary to open your food truck in a few months!

Figuring Out How to Find a Food Truck

We found our trailer on Gumtree. You will find most of the food trucks or trailers for sale on this website we mentioned before, which is the country's most common marketplace. You can also use the Facebook marketplace, which is growing exponentially or looking at Facebook groups dedicated to food truck owners.

Buying an Established Business, Is It for Me?

Sometimes owners sell their whole business with their food truck, meaning the entire concept: you take over their recipes, their locations, their regular customers, their social media. You won't start from scratch and take on a business that is already well established. This option is usually way more expensive than starting from scratch, but if you have the budget and the numbers they give you seem good, you can jump straight away! This can also be a good idea if you don't want to do all the administrative stuff, build your food truck, decorate it, etc. In this case, the past owner has already done everything, and there is nearly nothing to do. However, if you want to develop your idea, we recommend buying a «blank» food truck. Of course, this is a much longer process; you won't get immediately into the industry, and you'll have to work hard for it. But it is very rewarding and motivating to have your truck and develop your ideas! When we were looking for food trucks, business for sale cost $50000 minimum, and we couldn't afford it. We also wanted to have our menu, and our concept, a trailer to set up was the best solution!

Buying a New or a Second Hand Food Truck

Once again, this decision depends on your budget and what you want to do with your food truck. In Australia, the difference in price between a new vehicle and a second-hand one can be substantial.

1. *Buying a new food truck:* a new food truck will guarantee you more safety from a mechanical point of view and materials durability. Don't forget that the depreciation of value on a new vehicle is substantial; it will lose a large part of its value once you use it, and you'll have a hard time if you want to sell it at the same price you bought it. Depreciation is higher on a new food truck compared to a second hand one. We contacted companies that specialize in building custom-made food trucks, and they sent us estimations that could reach $100000!

2. *Buying a second-hand food truck:* buying a second-hand food truck will require work to adapt it to your specific project (buying appliances corresponding to the type of menu you want to offer) but will cost a lot less to buy. You can also hope to sell it more easily! This is the solution that we chose based on our budget and our project.

Costs of Equipment for an Empty Food Truck

We bought a food trailer from an Indian restaurant owner who was already using it as a food trailer on events. It was already well equipped and met most of the security standards. It already had a fridge, a microwave, a few utensils, and stainless-steel benches.

The electric system and plugs were already installed as well. This reduced our costs of equipment. Nevertheless, the inside was not well fitted out, and we could not adapt it exactly as we wanted.

If you buy an empty food truck, you will have to consider the time and money necessary to build it. You will have to install all the essential equipment for it to meet the standards: an electric system for the appliances and the lighting, sinks, and plumbing system, venting system on the roof, isolating materials for the walls and the floor, appliances, etc.

We spent around $7000 on top of the trailer's price to fit it out and decorate it. We added a venting system on the roof, an extra sink, a crepe machine, a kitchen robot, a raclette machine, the external painting and menus, a few utensils, and storage boxes.

Renting or Buying Your Food Truck?

Instead of buying your food truck, it is sometimes possible to rent one. It is not widely used, and we have not seen anyone doing it, but this could be an opportunity if you want to test the waters before really getting into the game. We met a few owners who were selling their food truck, and in the meantime, we're also renting it out. If you only find ads for food trucks for sale, do not hesitate to contact the seller to ask him if he would consider renting it. Some disadvantages can arise when renting a food truck. If you have to refuse events because the food truck is not available or have to get organized for two weeks in advance with the owner, this can become annoying! Buying your food truck allows you to be more flexible and do what you want when you want. It was important for us to acquire our food truck because we already had a concept in mind we wanted to develop ourselves. We thought about renting it while selling it (it took us several months to find a serious buyer). We finally decided to drop the idea as this would have required many administrative procedures (because the insurance and the trailer were registered in our name). The decoration was already painted on the food truck. It would also have been quite hard for others to adapt it to their specific needs.

Chapter 5. Layout Your kitchen

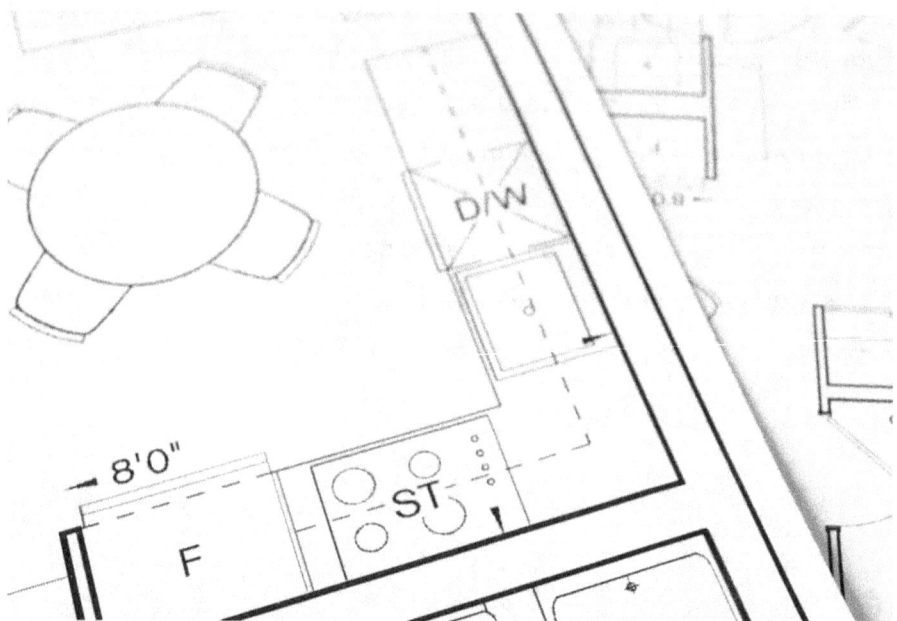

While some people say that food is the only important element in any food business, you know for a fact that it isn't true. Of course, it's also important for customers to be able to eat somewhere nice because no one really wants to eat in a truck that's rusty or that's not even designed at all.

If you don't have time to set up your truck in such a way that it would attract people, it may also mean that you are not yet ready for this business and that you may have to really think things through.

Anyway, there are some details to keep in mind when it comes to designing and decorating your food truck, such as the following:

44

The Theme

Suppose you're creating a burger business. It won't be right to use pastels as the theme or put photos of classic Hollywood stars on the walls of your truck, would it? You have to make sure that the theme you choose is connected to what you're serving so that your customers won't be confused.

Color Scheme

The main rule is to use the colors on the opposing sides of the color wheel. This way, everything will go together and your truck won't look like it's painted by a two-year-old. Also, it would be nice if the color scheme of your truck is also something you can use for the uniforms of you and your staff to make everything cohesive.

Seats

Some food trucks actually allow their customers to sit around the truck so if you can put out some chairs or anything where your customers can sit on, that would be good.

Utensils and Packaging

It would also be nice if you could set up the truck in such a way that your customers won't have a hard time getting the utensils they need. Always keep condiments and tissues around because most customers need them, and make sure that you have environment-friendly bags that they can just pick up and put their orders in so they can take them on the go.

And of Course, Give It Some Life

The best thing that you can do with your truck is put some of your personality in it. This way, your truck won't be generic and when people see it, they'll be excited to eat. When people notice that a food truck has life and that it's something cool, chances are they'll really go on and try your products—and that's something definitely good for you! Attract customers and they certainly will eat what you have prepared! Let your truck speak for itself.

What to Expect from a Custom Food Truck Builder

Custom food truck builders can be found in many major cities. However, their clients can be local or national, which helps expand your options when it comes to finding a builder for your project. Some of these companies ship custom food trucks to international locations as well.

Food truck builders usually offer full-service concept and design services for owners. These builders' job is to offer their expertise to help you design the perfect catering trailer or truck. They are also knowledgeable in building vehicles that adhere to

46

strict safety regulations. When employing a custom truck builder, you need to check out their previous projects and even talk to the owners of the trucks/trailers they've built to see if their customers are satisfied with the results.

Truck builders should be knowledgeable in safety and fire suppression systems, as well as servicing electrical wiring and connections. They should also be familiar with the various types of mobile kitchen equipment, as well as proper installation into a vehicle. Most custom truck builders should be able to take your project from start to finish depending on the services they offer. This is what you want to find because it's much easier to deal with one contact or company that can coordinate each phase of your vehicle build. This includes:

- Concept planning and design

- Electrical systems

- Fire systems

- Custom detailing services

- Graphic design

- Plumbing

- Vehicle wrap installation

- Equipment sales and installation

- And more

If you are working with an out-of-state builder, confirm they are familiar with the health codes and safety regulations for your city or state. Check to see if they've built vehicles that are operating in your state. In many cases, you may have to provide the specific rules and information to your builder.

Completion times can vary widely between different builders with some stating that they can finish builds in as little as 2 weeks. However, you should always expect delays and extended build times. These delays can come in many forms, including equipment permits, inspection scheduling, safety violations, equipment availability and more.

During the planning and building stage, it's a good idea to imagine being inside the truck preparing meals to identify where the bottlenecks might occur. Arrange to personally inspect and evaluate the interior during the build phase. Every piece of equipment you put into your truck takes up valuable space. The last surprise you want is realizing that you placed a grill or cooler unit in the wrong spot after your truck or trailer has been delivered to you.

Vehicle Wrap and Exterior Design

It's actually astonishing how much money can be spent building the interior of your food truck. Installing the necessary equipment with an efficient layout is a major part of a step van conversion. However, the exterior of your vehicle requires just as much thought and planning. With your mobile food business, you only get one chance to create a great first impression... This happens long before a customer has even ordered food from your truck. Within the first few seconds of seeing your truck, potential customers will immediately make decisions of whether or not they will order food from you. They may buy from you at that moment or their first visit could come days or weeks later because they remembered your truck design.

Your vehicle wrap alone can single-handedly convey the overall tone and style of your mobile food business to your customers. Marketing experts have shown that vehicle wraps are noticed and remembered better in almost all types of advertising, except for TV ads. In terms of expenses, designing and wrapping can cost somewhere between $3,000 and $5,000.

Your graphics should be bright and easy to read. The goal is to help bring attention to your truck and hopefully attract more customers. The vehicle wrap literally turns your vehicle into a mobile billboard that can express the atmosphere around your truck and give a sense of the type of food you serve as well as your contact information. Your wrap is one of the most important components of your brand. The 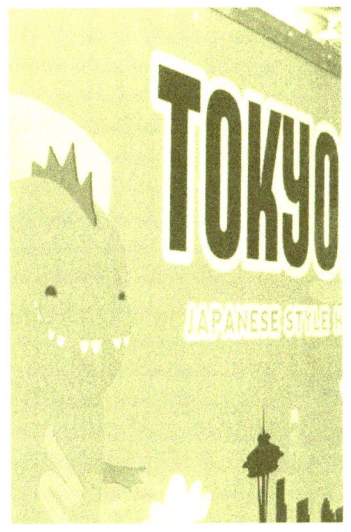 graphics on your wrap can then be incorporated into other elements of your marketing materials. This includes graphics for your website and packagings like cups, napkins, business cards and more. According to some, one of the downsides of vehicle wraps is that the adhesives used on the vinyl panels only last about 5 years when exposed to the outdoor elements. However, that time frame is just an estimate and your wrap could stay intact much longer. If you operate in a metropolitan area with lots of high buildings, consider extending your wrap to the roof so that people looking down on the street can recognize your truck.

Regarding contact information on your vehicle wrap, be sure to also include your website address, Facebook and Twitter tags on the sides and back panels of your food truck. The exterior without a doubt is the most visible part of your business, so it's worth including your company details on the side. Keep your contact information large enough to be readable from a moderate distance but don't let it distract customers from your main logo and brand graphics.

If you want to save money on your exterior graphics, you don't have to wrap the entire vehicle. You can instead have just your logos printed on large vinyl sheets that act like giant stickers your installer can adhere to the sides of your vehicle. If you want to coordinate the base color of your vehicle with your logo, consider having the exterior of your truck painted a single color before adding your vinyl logos and contact information.

Power Generators and Propane

When you're out on the streets, your truck needs to be self-sufficient. Every piece of equipment needs to be able to run on its own without a tether to hard-line power sources and gas resources. This is accomplished with propane tanks and electrical generators. Every food truck needs both to be able to operate unless you are at a food truck park or other venue with available shore power and gas hook-ups.

Portable generators supply the electricity to your onboard appliances which include refrigerators, toasters, waffle irons, blenders, payment systems and more. Some trucks have compartments designed specifically to house power generators and keep them out of sight and to reduce noise. Food trucks that do not built-in enclosures will have power generators placed next to their trucks with power lines connected through ports on the side of the vehicle.

Determining the size of a generator (wattage) you need depends on the equipment you have on-board. The best way to do this is simply to take inventory of all the electrical appliances you will be using. Then add up the wattage or amperes (amps) required by all of your appliances. You'll also need to know which appliances you'll be using simultaneously to avoid overloading your generator during your preparation and food service.

Total wattage in an appliance is calculated using this equation:

$$Watts = Amps \times Volts$$

For example, if your device is rated at 5 amps and 120 volts, the wattage requirements of that device are 600 watts (5A x 120V = 600 Watts).

Sudden Power Surges

After you've made your calculations, add up the total wattage to help you choose the right generator for your truck. To avoid potential shut-downs, you will need to anticipate some extra available wattage use when choosing a generator. Some appliances will draw more power on startup or at different intervals so you will need extra capacity for that. Fortunately, most generators have a surge or peak power rating. The peak power rating indicates the amount of additional wattage the generator can produce for very short periods of time.

A sudden draw of power may happen when you start any electrical appliance. For example, a refrigerator may require 2200 watts to start its compressor (starting wattage) and then 700 watts to run after that (running wattage). When you add up your wattage requirements, you need to use the starting wattage in your calculations.

It's a fact that running a generator creates a lot of noise, not to mention the exhaust fumes. Most food truck owners will place their generators on the opposite side of their vehicle away from the service window to keep noise to a minimum for their customers. Some food truck owners may even use two generators at the same time. But be aware that you will need to haul these heavy machines in and out of your truck each time you use them unless they're mounted in a compartment on your vehicle.

Propane Tanks

While it is vital to know the electrical requirements of your appliances, you will also need to be able to anticipate the amount of propane you will need for your truck so you won't run out at the busiest time! Propane tanks have approximate BTU ratings that you will use along with the BTU ratings of your gas appliances to help determine how long a propane tank will supply gas to your truck. The BTU ratings on an appliance assume that you will be operating the appliance at 100%. For example, the calculations are made on gas grills with all burners set on high or a water heater set at the maximum temperature.

If you don't know the size of your tank, first you need to measure the height and diameter of your propane tank. Do not include the height of the collar at the bottom (and top) of the tank. The collar is just used as a base to keep the tank upright. The diameter is measured at the widest point of the tank. Here are some common tank sizes to help determine the capacity of a new or existing tank:

20lb tank = 18 inches high x 12.5 inch diameter

30lb tank = 24 inches high x 12.5 inch diameter

40lb tank = 29 inches high x 12.5 inch diameter

100lb tank = 48 inches high x 14.5 inch diameter

Once you know the tank size, you can then determine the BTU capacity when it is full. The following list displays the BTU capacity of the various tank sizes:

20lb tank = 430,270 BTU

30lb tank = 649,980 BTU

40lb tank = 860,542 BTU

100lb tank = 2,160,509 BTU

Next, you need to find all the BTU ratings of your propane-powered equipment. You can usually find the BTU rating stamped or printed on the appliance itself. If you can't find the rating on the appliance, you will have to consult the owner's manual or contact the manufacturer. If you purchase new equipment, it's a good idea to keep all your manuals in a safe place for future reference.

After you have added up the BTU ratings of your gas appliances, divide this number with your propane tank BTU number to calculate the number of hours your propane tank will be able to supply fuel to your appliances at 100%. Every truck has different equipment on-board so there are no standard figures to go by. But you can estimate your usage by doing research on specific gas-powered appliances you plan to put into operation to help determine the tank size your truck will require.

Propane Tank Safety

To avoid potential problems with your propane tanks, keep the hoses that run from the tank to your truck secured. Do not leave hoses which are too long to sway freely with vehicle movement. The tanks on the outside of the vehicle need to be shielded from damage. Usually, a steel cage can be placed around a tank. A leak indicator mounted inside the vehicle is also a great way to help prevent potentially dangerous incidents that can occur with these highly pressurized tanks.

A final note about propane tanks, they need to be securely mounted to your vehicle. These external propane tanks are also prone to damage in a vehicle accident and can cause dangerous situations on the streets. Protective covers may be required by local regulations before you can drive with on-board propane tanks. Many food truck owners mount their tanks on the rear of the vehicle while others can be mounted

underneath. If mounting underneath, a saddle mount or horizontal mount tank will be required. Trailers often have tanks secured on the trailer tongue that connects to a hitch.

Plumbing and Water System

Another vital component of your food truck is the water system. At the heart of the water system is the built-in water tank. The water tanks in today's food trucks provide the same quality standards as those found in a restaurant sink. Water holding tanks have to be FDA approved in order for a food truck to pass inspection. There are strict requirements specifying that holding tanks must be constructed of strong materials and be easy to clean. Typical water tanks used in food trucks are made from non-corrosive polyethylene plaster resin. This is the same material used in kitchen tools. like plastic bowls and other plastic utensils.

Seamless water tanks constructed of one piece of plastic are the most effective at preventing leaks. It's also a good idea to consider a water tank which has UV protection to help avoid premature aging and cracking when exposed to sunlight. It's almost impossible to visually tell if the plastic water tank is brittle; so, the UV option can help prevent unexpected damage and prolong the life of your water system.

Fresh Water Tanks

Fresh water typically travels from the water tank to the faucets via an on-demand pump. This means the pump only runs when the valve is open on your faucet. These pumps run on electricity, so its wattage must be accounted for with the generator you are using. Some trucks and trailers have fresh water tanks mounted up high on a wall or ceiling allowing gravity to move water to your faucet. However, always check with your local health department to verify that you are installing your plumbing equipment to comply with codes.

As a responsible food truck owner, you must clean and sanitize water tanks on a regular basis to avoid contamination and foodborne illness. Because water tanks are meant to be used over a short period of time, they must be refilled regularly to help prevent problems related to standing water and bacteria growth.

Hot Water System

Hot running water is a necessity in any foodservice business. In a food truck, hot water must be generated inside the vehicle. Not only is it used for cooking, hot water is required for washing dirty utensils and cooking equipment. Water systems in food trucks use water heaters to produce hot water, just like in homes or other businesses.

Water heaters used in foodservice vehicles are usually electrically powered. They are easy to install and efficient. They have reservoirs of varying capacities, which could be an issue if you choose a water heater which is too small. There are also tankless models that generate hot water on demand. Tankless models are also powered by electricity but provide generous amounts of hot water as long as you have reserves in your fresh water tanks.

There are also water heaters that run on gas. This is great for reducing the load on your generator but it also introduces another issue. Gas water heaters need to be vented outside because of dangerous carbon monoxide fumes. A gas water heater requires a special enclosure to isolate fumes from the interior airspace of the truck. Gas water heaters can heat up water fast but may require additional attention by inspectors.

Sink Requirements

When it comes to sink requirements, food trucks must follow closely to the same standards that brick-and-mortar restaurants adhere to. Those basic policies require the installation of sinks with

58

at least three compartments plus a hand-washing sink. The three-compartment sinks are used for manually washing, rinsing and sanitizing the utensils, cooking equipment and tableware on-board your vehicle. Also, these sinks must be large to accommodate the biggest pieces of cooking equipment, like pots and pans.

Properly designed sink systems have areas for rinsing and scraping food into garbage receptacles. After scraping left-over food off of utensils and other kitchen tools, items must be washed with detergent in the first sink compartment.

Water temperatures in the first compartment should be at least 110 degrees Fahrenheit. After prolonged use, the water and detergent must be replaced when suds are no longer present or the water appears dirty.

The second compartment is used for rinsing items after they've been washed. The water must be clean to remove all detergent and food particles when items are immersed.

The third compartment will sanitize the items that have been washed and rinsed. Hot water or chemical sanitizer can be used in this step. However, if plain hot water is to be used, it must be at least 171°C (340°F) and items need to be submerged in the hot water for at least 30 seconds. Finally, all items that have been washed, rinsed and sanitized should be air-dried on a clean drain board.

The handwashing sink is obviously for washing your hands and is smaller in size than the three-compartment sinks. All food handlers are required to wash hands before touching or preparing any food. Frequent handwashing helps prevent cross-contamination when working with food.

Grey Water Tank

The water you drain out of your sinks is called grey water and it must be stored on your vehicle until you can get to an approved disposal station. This water cannot legally be dumped in a storm or sewer drain. The grey water contains grease and food particles and must be disposed of properly. The facilities that accept grey water must have grease interceptors in place and be approved by the health department.

Grey water tanks need to be 15% larger than your fresh water tanks. That's because the waste water contains extra materials such as food waste which will take up more room in the tank. In addition, you may be dumping other liquids in your sinks like beverages and ice that will also drain into the grey water tanks. Most grey water tanks on food trucks and trailers are mounted underneath the vehicle (if there's space) so it doesn't take up additional room in the kitchen area. Others may mount these tanks under sinks inside the vehicle.

When building a food truck, take into consideration how much fresh water you will use before choosing a size. Sometimes truck builders will recommend fresh and grey water tanks that are much larger than you actually need. This not only increases your expenses but also the additional water contributes significant weight to your vehicle. Just for your reference, 1 gallon of water equals approximately 8 pounds.

Typical sizes for water tanks in a single foodservice vehicle are:

30-35 gallon fresh water

50-55 gallon grey water

Though tank sizes can vary, your local city or county health department may have minimum size requirements specifically for your vehicle. Whether it's fresh water or grey water, you must have an adequate supply and capacity so you don't run into issues during your service times.

Venting and Fire Suppression

If you are cooking inside your vehicle, regulations require to have a vent system, which consists of two parts: The vent hood and the exhaust fan. Vent hoods are mounted over the cooking area such as a stove or griddle. In a foodservice vehicle, they are typically placed closer to the cooking surface than in a brick-and-mortar restaurant because of lower ceiling clearance. Hoods are often custom built to fit the exact width over the cooking area inside your vehicle. Custom truck builders can fabricate these units in their shops and install them as part of the food truck conversion process. Vent hoods are often made of stainless steel and integrated with a custom fabricated work surface where your cooking equipment will be mounted.

The second part of the venting system includes an exhaust fan mounted on the exterior of the vehicle... usually on the roof right above the vent hood. The cooking fumes are channeled out of the vehicle from ducting connected to the vent hood. Duct and exhaust fan sizes for your vehicle are determined by the type of cooking equipment that will be installed.

Running an exhaust fan usually requires a 120-volt electrical power source. So again take note of the wattage the fan needs in order to run. During your food service, cooking creates steam and vaporized grease, which is sucked out of the vehicle by the exhaust fan. This airborne mixture can cause a mess. Over time, this exhaust can condense and create sludge. Because of this, exhaust fans have built-in grease cups to prevent excess grease from collecting and dripping onto your vehicle.

Exhaust systems must be regularly inspected for grease build-up to help prevent issues like fires. Inspections are typically required on a monthly basis for businesses that burn fuel like charcoal or wood-burning ovens.

Fire Suppression Equipment

An integral part of food truck safety involves the fire suppression system built into the vehicle. Fire suppression equipment is required on all foodservice vehicles. Like brick-and-mortar restaurants, hot cooking surfaces, open flames, oils, chemicals and electrical connections all create a volatile situation that can cause small flames to quickly get out of control. Any fire in and around your vehicle can cause significant expense or bodily injury to those nearby. This can devastate your business and close you down for good.

An automatic fire suppression system is required before your truck can be put into operation. That's because about 60% of all restaurant fires involve hot cooking equipment. Automatic systems can suppress flames with chemicals and automatically shut down gas lines. The fire system can also shut off electricity, which could further fuel the fire or cause additional dangers. While approval is needed before you go into operation, your fire suppression system is also required to have semi-annual inspections to verify that it will function correctly when needed.

Secondary Fire Extinguishers

A secondary fire extinguisher to keep on your vehicle is a Class ABC. This type of extinguisher is mainly used for non-grease fires from paper, plastics, wood and electrical sources. It's good policy to have a Class ABC extinguisher stored inside the cab of the vehicle as well as the kitchen area. Make sure all persons working in the vehicle know the location and operation of fire systems and extinguishers.

In the event of a fire, you should have an evacuation plan in place right from the launch of your business. Fire suppression systems can buy you time to escape your vehicle. But getting out as quickly as possible should be your first priority. In case of fire, call 911 and do not re-enter your vehicle until fire officials deem it safe.

Equipment Costs

When starting your research, it can be difficult to find information to help you calculate the cost of building a food truck. In this section, you'll find different types of equipment with approximate costs to help you get a better idea of the startup costs as it relates to equipping your food truck. The approximate costs listed below are in USD.

Equipment	Estimated Cost
Water System	$4200
Propane System	$4000
Exhaust Hood	$3500
Generator Compartment	$1200
Fire Suppression System	$3200
Interior Sliding Window	$700
19 cu. ft. Refrigerator-Freezer	$750
Small Freezer	$430
27" Sandwich Fridge	$2400
48" Sandwich Fridge	$3400
60" Sandwich Fridge	$3700
Single Door Cooler	$1400
Double Door Cooler	$2600
Full Size Steamer-Warmer	$1400
Double Steamer-Warmer	$2800
Triple Steamer-Warmer	$4200
24" Range	$4100
36" Range	$4600
2 Burner Stove Top	$1100
4 Burner Stove Top	$1800

Equipment	Estimated Cost
6 Burner Stove Top	$4000
18" Griddle	$1600
24" Griddle	$2300
36" Griddle	$2800
48" Griddle	$3200
18" Char Broiler	$1700
24" Char Broiler	$2100
36" Char Broiler	$2700
48" Char Broiler	$3000
Wall Mounted Potato Cutter	$380
Double Crepe Griddles	$2200
Gyro Machine	$2800
40lb Two Basket Deep Fryer	$1900
Pizza Oven	$6000

As you can see, your costs can add up pretty fast even with just minimal cooking equipment on board your truck. The approximate prices listed above are for new items only. But you can find good deals on used equipment from websites like eBay or Craigslist.

Chapter 6. How to Create the Right Food Truck Menu

There are numerous fundamental segments of your food truck business, however none more significant than your menu. Clients are at last going to pass judgment on you on how delicious your menu is. Your menu decides how fruitful you'll be and what level of administration you can accommodate your clients. A very much planned menu will leave clients hungry for more and diminishes the weight on your shoulders.

An inadequately planned menu will destroy your business before it even gets off the ground. First-time food truck proprietors will probably lose track of the main issue at hand when arranging their menus. In the surge of beginning another endeavor, they will probably go out and purchase the most costly fixings, which will build their expenses. Subsequently, they'll value themselves out of the market. You can't contend with fancy eateries from a food truck. So don't think you need to have the best fixings.

This doesn't mean your fixings should not be right. You need to stick to a meaningful boundary someplace and offset your longings with reasonableness. Less expensive meat and more affordable vegetables can be similarly as delicious as the more costly ones. You need to get imaginative with how you cook them. Remembering the motivation behind a food truck, ensure your menu has a brisk turnaround time.

General Tips

Speedy turnaround times are critical for food trucks since clients won't stick around until the end of time. They're probably going to line outside an eatery that serves brilliant food, yet this isn't the situation with a food truck. Buyers have numerous different alternatives that it doesn't bode well for them to do as such. In case you're focusing on the noon office swarm, nobody will remain around for over 10 minutes to get their food.

Conceptualize dishes that can be set up ahead of time and be assembled or food that prepares rapidly. If your foods contain rice in them, this is something you can get ready well ahead of time. Staying with the Mexican food model, you would have to gather a burrito or a taco with cooked fixings to deliver a flavorful dish. Different cooking styles loan themselves to such associations too.

Another terrific method to decrease your costs is to make a menu that uses a standard arrangement of fixings. Only one out of every odd dish on your menu needs similar fixings; however, restrict them to a modest number. This makes looking for fixings significantly simpler. By purchasing a greater amount of fixings, you can get them in mass, diminishing your expenses. It additionally decreases the odds of food going to squander since your segments will be used in each dish.

Remember that quality must be superior to quantity. Your clients aren't anticipating a café, so don't think you need to give them a wide range of food. Adhere to the ones you can cook well and that they'll cherish. Furthermore, remember my past point about changing menus with the seasons. This allows you to invigorate your menu so you won't be stuck cooking very similar foods the entire year.

Your expenses influence your costs. On the off likelihood that you follow the past tips, you'll naturally have the option to set sensible prices that convey your clients' incentive. Remember you're maintaining a business. Clients will consistently go to whichever spot gives them the most noteworthy worth. Your food may taste extraordinary, however, there's the most excellent value somebody will pay for it. So, don't let your inner self set costs. Follow the tips in this part to set sensible prices and consistently keep your expenses as low as you can.

Menu Themes and Space Considerations

When picking the cooking for your food truck, it very well may be challenging to choose which one to select. I've just referenced how you need to approach narrowing down your alternatives. On the off chance that numerous trucks serve your food style, you can discover either specialty down or change the kind of cooking you need to do. Choose the topic of your menu and begin narrowing it down from that point.

Each food truck has certain central items which will be arranged the most and pass on all that your vehicle has to bring to the table. They should be intently attached to the topic of your cooking. They additionally should be anything but difficult to cook and shouldn't need your clients to stand by in long queues. This is a tough task. You could cook those items in advance and store them in warm holders before serving.

Be reasonable about the number of options that can be on your menu. You'll be working with a little staff (generally only two persons, including yourself), and you'll be working in a more modest space. Regardless of how huge your business kitchen space is, you will serve food out of your truck. You'll have to convey incredible taste to your clients. It's an extreme task, so ensure you set aside the effort to contemplate your menu.

The more modest your menu is, the higher its quality must be. Nonetheless, you would prefer not to go excessively little since this will dismiss clients. If this is your first time maintaining a business, save it under ten dishes for the wellbeing of your own. Whenever you've arrived at a couple of options, it's an ideal opportunity to test it out. Have your staff and family taste your dishes and time how many minutes it requires for you to serve them. Attempt to cook the dishes 30 seconds quicker and check whether this is conceivable.

In a genuine climate, you'll probably have not so much time but rather more pressure. This is the reason the 30-second test is a decent one to reach. It trains you to move quicker, so when the genuine article comes, you'll be available. Gather criticism from every individual who tastes your menu and fuse it. On the off chance your food isn't ready, endure it, and update your menu. Try not to adhere to your old menu obstinately.

Joining criticism into your choices is the way to prevailing around here. You should be imaginative and make money. You'll probably need to experience a couple of emphases of your menu before you land on the ideal blend. Smooth out your alternatives however much as could be expected. In case you're serving grains, restrict them to two prospects. In case you're serving wraps, limit the number of items your clients can add.

You need to find some kind of harmony between smoothing out and offering no choices by any stretch of the imagination, so be cautious about this. Look for criticism from the people around you and consolidate it into your plans. Whenever you've arrived at a triumphant mix, it's an ideal opportunity to value your food.

Choose Your Cuisine

International influences are and always have been a major force in the development of American cuisine.

American diners regularly prove their interest in encountering and trying out culinary traditions from around the world, venturing past their "usual" foreign cuisine picks and sampling less-familiar dishes in an effort to expand their palates and discover new favorites.

American Cuisine

Attempting to characterize American food could be testing because of flavors from the mixture of conventional American cooking procedures blended in with flavors from different societies. While there is, by all accounts, a mainstream misinterpretation that cheeseburgers and franks rule our taste buds, our cooking has much more to bring to the table. There is a bounty of fish dishes including lobster and shellfishes, and Louisiana's Cajun and Creole foods, which are dishes arranged with bunches of hot sauces and fish. We should not disregard America's breadbasket in the Midwest with apparently perpetual corn, soy, and wheat fields. We can't forego customary dishes, for example, turkey and crusty fruit-filled treat.

Pioneers, pilgrims, and migrants presented a lot of fixings and plans. Sorts of American Cuisine incorporates wieners, cheeseburgers, pizza, BBQ, roasted chicken, French fries, macaroni, thus substantially more!

71

Asian Cuisine

For what reason is it a smart thought to purchase an Asian Cuisine Food Truck?

We live in an energizing time for Asian cooking business people. Somewhere in the range of 1999 and 2015, deals of Asian cheap food rose 135%. Starting in 2019, there were very nearly 20 million Asian-Americans in the United States... yet stand by! You mustn't have Asian blood to like Asian food. Asian cooking is mainstream, and it is no big surprise for Asian cooking food trucks. You are moving.

<u>Various Styles of Asian Food</u>

- *Southwestern Asian Food – India, Pakistan, Sri Lanka, Myanmar*

  This district's food is intensely affected by creamed sauces dependent on dairy, yogurt, curries, solid flavors, and level pieces of bread.

- *Northeastern Asian Food – China, Korea, Japan*

  The nourishments in this locale are cooked with fats, oils, flavors, spoonfuls of vinegar, and soy. Noodles are a prevailing starch.

- *Southeastern Asian Food – Thailand, Laos, Cambodia, Vietnam, Indonesia, Malaysia, Singapore, Brunei*

This territory brings us new, fragrant, daintily arranged food. Discrete flavors are utilized with traces of citrus and spices. Fish sauce for soy. Curries dependent on coconut milk.

French Cuisine

Over time, French food was affected by the many encompassing societies of Spain, Italy, Switzerland, Germany, and Belgium. French foods have a special style of cooking. They are broadly known as craftsmanship food due to their magnificence, flavor, therapeutic planning, and introduction.

Indian Cuisine

It is safe to say that you are energetic about Indian food flavors and plans? Is it safe to say that you are one of those home culinary experts who is constantly celebrated by loved ones? Perhaps it is time you dare to begin your Indian Food Truck and bring in cash for accomplishing something you love. Additionally, you will find the opportunity to carry your delectable food to the world! Since food trucks have picked up so much notoriety, numerous Indian Restaurants have extended their blocks and mortar area by going portable with an Indian Food Truck.

Beyond question, food trucks are a tremendous piece of our way of life at this moment. The extraordinary Indian culture and Indian food can be communicated in an Indian Food Truck. If it's a curry in a rush that you relish, from Mumbai road food works of art like

Pani puri or vada pav or your standard Americanized works of art like margarine chicken.

Italian Cuisine

What makes Italian cooking mainstream and adored by everybody? It's the flavor, quality, and straightforward fixings that play into its notoriety. It is extraordinary to put into an Italian food truck or trailer because of the assortment of dishes you can serve and their popularity. Investigate some of the Italian cooking food trucks and trailers and get enlivened! The next Italian trailer or food truck in town could be yours!

Latin Cuisine

Got some Latin soul in you? Latin cooking has been developing ubiquity in the United States.

It isn't only the common Mexican food with the well-known taco truck, yet also the kinds of numerous others including empanadas, arepas, average Cuban dishes, ceviches, and tostones rellenos, and ordinary treats, among others.

Mediterranean Cuisine

Greek Food Trucks are very well known because Mediterranean cooking is the most loved style of food. The food truck industry is developing, and expected to keep on developing.

Five Advice to Create a Perfect Food Truck Menu

You might have the best food in town, but if customers don't order it, your food truck is doomed. That's why it's so important to make sure your menu is the best it can be. Taking a few simple steps to plan, organize, and design your food truck menu can make a world of difference to your mobile food business' success. Here are 5 advices that can help you take your food truck menu board to the next level:

1. Incorporate a Popular Meal

It's always a good idea to have a meal that most people are used to because you never know who is going to order at your truck—this popular item might stand out to them!

2. Go Outside of Your Concept

It's okay to go outside of your concept from time to time! This is your kitchen, and your business, so if you want to cook something that doesn't exactly relate to your food concept, then by all means do so! You're the boss! Just mark up this meal as a special, or only offer it for a limited time.

3. Get Seasonal with Your Menu

If you want to attract customers year-round, then you might have to get seasonal with your menu. Now, you don't have to change up your entire menu but it would be wise to add a couple of different meals for the winter and summer. For example, incorporate some type of soup in the winter (or comfort food), and then add a cold dessert in the summer!

4. **Don't Forget About the Beverage Department**

It is perfectly fine to have a soda/pop machine in your mobile kitchen, it would also be wise to concoct some homemade drinks. Being unique and standing out is the name of the game in this industry, so make sure to add some unique drinks to your menu!

5. **Always Add Your Own Unique Twist**

You want to stand out in the food truck industry, which is why you should always add your own unique twist to your meals. There is an endless amount of ways to spice up meals, and you surely can add your own unique twist to even the most common meals.

Setting Prices

Costs are a critical part of your business. They decide your benefit rate and pass on the level of significant worth you're giving your clients. You need your expenses to create the perfect measure of benefit for yourself and leave you a sufficient cradle to, in any event, equal the initial investment if things turn out badly. The standard methodology is to increase the unit cost of an item by three to show up at the selling cost.

Request likewise assumes a job. If your truck turns out to be notable for a specific dish, you can charge more for it. If you've seen that a specific dish is popular at a particular time or because of the scene you're in, you can raise costs. You would prefer not to coerce your clients, be reasonable with your cost increments.

Cafés additionally use a food cost rate model. Regularly, the food's cost is somewhere in the range of 20 and 40% of the deal cost. If a menu item costs $2 to set up, its deal cost can be between $5 to $10—the 3X increase lands in this reach. It would be best if you incremented or lessened your expenses, relying upon the amount of time it requires to set up a thing.

This strategy puts a premium on your gross edges (recall them?) Your gross edge is determined as follows:

Stage 1

Sale cost ($5.00) - cost ($1.00) = $4.00

Stage 2

Divide the result of Step 1 by Sale cost → 4/5 = 0.8 = 80%

You need your gross edges to be as high as conceivable since this gives you more space to represent working costs. Notwithstanding, you can't push prices just so high before clients rebel. You'll see that in the wake of representing reasonable client costs, your gross edges will land around 40-80%. If your gross advantages are not as much as this, you need to have low working costs. A frozen yogurt distributing truck will have low operational expenses since there isn't a lot of prep work that should be done other than making huge bunches and putting away items. A vehicle that prepares new food will have higher working costs since stock turnover will be quicker.

You can target food expenses to be a certain level of your menu cost. Suppose you need food expenses to be 30% of your menu value (which implies your gross edge is 70%), and a dish costs you $2 to make. Its deal cost is determined as:

Menu cost = Cost value/Cost rate = 2/0.3 = $6.66

Another method of moving toward menu evaluation is to focus on a gross edge and see what costs you end up with. Suppose a menu item costs you $2 to plan, and you need to acquire half gross advantages on this dish. The deal cost can be determined as:

Net edge sum wanted = Cost value/Gross edge percent = 2/0.5 = $4

Menu cost = cost + Gross edge cost = 4+2 = $6

You'll have to check whether this item can sensibly sell for $6 per ration. If it's a plate of fries, nobody will pay this much for them. If it's a burger, it's a take. Food cost rates and gross edges are two of a kind. They add together to give you your last menu cost.

Chapter 7. How to Write a Business Plan

We will go over the actual steps of forming your food truck business plan. But first, let's define what a business plan is. In essence, a business plan explains in detail how you will operate your commerce. A good business plan helps you organize all aspects of running your business right from the very beginning! If you've never transcribed a business plan before, you're not alone. A lot of people need help or are unsure of what to include in such a plan. Don't worry if you tumble into that category! It's not that complicated!

Generally, a food truck business plan can contain a list of locations where you plan on parking to attract customers. A list of your food suppliers can also be included, so you'll know exactly where your ingredients will come from. It's also a good idea to list alternate suppliers too! A business plan can spell out your source of funding. Most likely, funding will come from a bank, but other methods can also be listed. You must also include estimates of how much it will cost for you to start your business. Expenses for the first few months of operations can be included here as well. You can add other items depending on your needs. However, this is just a simple overview to help you write your business plan.

An essential aspect of a business plan is that it's not locked in stone. Your business plan can be improved as your business grows and expands.

What to Include in Your Business Plan

At this instant, you may be questioning: *"What specifically needs to be included in a business plan?"*

First of all, you need an executive summary, which is an executive summary, a brief overview of your business.

It explains the purpose of your business. It also explains what you want to achieve with your business. What are your future goals?

You'll must do competitive analysis as well. This will help you understand and know who your competition will be. Are there other trucks in your city serving the same type of food as yours? The competitive analysis can give you insight into what makes your competition so successful in your city or region. Proper research can help reveal the strengths and weaknesses of the competition. By knowing what your competition is doing, you can adapt and do something better with your truck. This can help you develop something new that the competition doesn't have.

Besides, you must include your product offerings too. This consists of a detailed list of your menu items. You should explain why you chose to put these items on the menu. Write down how your food will be prepared. This will also help you decide what type of equipment you will need. Your business plan will also include an industry analysis. In your case, you could explain the growing popularity of the food truck industry and why you want to be a portion of it. The industry analysis should also explain how you'll compete with other food trucks in your area. You might also want to include any relevant facts and statistics about this industry in this part.

Another part of your business idea should include sales and marketing information. This will spell out your promotion and marketing plans. As part of sales and marketing, explain your social media strategy. This will include the development of your website, which is an important marketing tool in and of itself. It would be best to document other marketing efforts, such as e-mail marketing used very successfully in different industries for years. You can also list locations, events, festivals, and venues you plan on attending. When preparing your sales and marketing analysis, you should compare your prices against your competition's prices.

Additional Business Plan Info

Moving away from sales and marketing, you must also explain your management structure. Clearly describe the primary individuals' roles so that there's no question of each person's business duties. You must also list your day-to-day operations and explain how the daily tasks will be accomplished. For example, information listed in the day-to-day operations can explain where you will be preparing your food. This could be a commercial kitchen or directly inside the truck. Also, in your daily operations, you should explain when and where you will buy your ingredients.

As part of your business plan, it is vital to make some financial projections and include practical information on how you plan to become profitable. These projections will help you estimate when you will become profitable by paying off your startup expenses.

You should prepare a cash and balance sheet estimate for the first year, so you know exactly where your money is coming from and where it is spent. When preparing your financial projections, don't overestimate your profit potential. All this information will help you determine your financial requirements to estimate how much financing you will need. The amount of funding required is based on the information you entered for your profit and expense estimates.

Describe how and where you will invest your money. Please include how much of your own money you will support, if any. Please note that loans are more likely to be approved if you invest some of your own money. Also, you should include any other relevant documentation you feel will be helpful. This can consist of licenses, permits, awards, and diplomas. And to reiterate, it is imperative not to exaggerate any figures or documentation in your estimates. Remember to include any relevant information that clearly explains your operations and expects to make a profit.

To help you build your business plan, it might help research existing plans in similar industries to get ideas on how to develop your project. Writing your business plan is the first building block of your business. Investors and financial institutions like banks will be looking closely at your plan to determine if you're worthy of financial help.

Food Truck Business Plan – Basic Structure

Executive Summary

Introduce the name of your food truck and what you plan to serve. It summarizes a longer report or proposal in such a way that readers can rapidly become acquainted with a large body of material without having to read it all.

Mission Statement

This should be a short description of the mission of your business. A mission statement works best if you print a copy of it to keep inside your food truck. This statement should guide the decisions of your business.

Company Concept/Description

Write what you hope the food truck will become, the food you plan to serve, and why you believe it will be a successful business.

Market Analysis

Get an understanding of your local competition. What other food trucks are successful in your town? How do you intend to create a unique offering in your market?

Management Structure

This is a brief section for most food trucks. Write down who will be participating in the business and the specific responsibilities of each team member.

Product Line

In the case of a food truck, publish your menu here.

Sales and Marketing

Write down how you plan to market your business and generate sales. Figuring out specific places you plan to sell is really important for food trucks in this section.

Funding Request

Share how much money you'll need to start the business and list out exactly how you plan to spend each dollar. Buying the food truck or trailer will be the biggest startup expense.

Financial Projections

Share how much you plan to make.

Appendix

Include any supplemental information here. Ideas include a copy of your business and health department permits, photos of the truck, or anything else you think would be beneficial.

Startup Expenses

As part of the business plan process, you'll need to come up with your startup costs. It's in your best interest to be as detailed as possible when figuring out your total costs by line item so you're not surprised. Your startup cash is extremely valuable. You should not overspend on equipment or anything else you don't need. Eliminating unnecessary equipment gives you more space for storage, which is extremely valuable on a food truck.

Below are some of the most common startup expenses for a food truck business:

Food Truck Start-up Costs		
Equipment	**Estimated Cost**	**Notes**
Food Truck	$5,000 - $125,000	Feel free to add your personal notes here
Initial Product Inventory	$1,000-$2,000	
Permits and Licenses	$100-$500	Varies a lot depending on where you operate

Food Truck Start-up Costs		
Equipment	**Estimated Cost**	**Notes**
Website	$0-$5,000	Varies a lot depending on what you want
Social network	$0-$500	Varies a lot depending on you ADS
Register/POS	$200-$1,000	Can also use an iPad and an app for credit transactions
Uniforms/T-Shirts	$0-$1,000	
Paper Products (Plates/Napkins, etc.)	$200-$300	
Misc. Expenses (Like a Chalk Menu)	$500-$2000	Plan for some unexpected expenses here and put it into the budget
Small wares: Pots, Pans, etc.	$1000-$2000	
TOTAL	**$8,000-$139,300**	

Food Truck On-Going Costs		
Item	**Monthly Estimated Cost**	**Notes**
Fuel	$500	This will vary a lot
Commissary	$500-$2,000	Some counties require food trucks to park overnight at safe place
Labor	???	$8-$15 per hour is average rate
Repairs	$1,000	Better to budget for it

Food Truck On-Going Costs		
Item	**Monthly Estimated Cost**	**Notes**
Food/Beverage Restock	???	Depends on food cost and frequency of operation
Paper Product Restock	???	Depends on food cost and frequency of operation
Insurance	$50-$150	
TOTAL	**???**	

Chapter 8. How to Market Your Product

Social media is a must. Facebook, Instagram, Twitter, LinkedIn, Snapchat and Tik Tok: with each of these you can reach your guests in different ways or reach a different demographic!

Some of the most successful truck food entrepreneurs are the ones who are making use of social media opportunities to connect with their customers and generate buzz. You can keep followers informed of your location through your feed, and use social networks to attract new customers. Other tools give you an opportunity to interact with your fans and supporters by allowing them to vote on new menu items, choose the color of your truck before you repaint, or pick your next weekly special.

Taking photos of your food, your set up and your specials is an easy daily post. Remember, social media is a conversation between you and your guests. If they talk to you via comments, you MUST respond; otherwise, it is like hanging up on a guest with hundreds or thousands of folks watching.

Use Facebook Business to create ads that are posted on timelines. You pay for only the amount of exposure you can afford. Facebook often sets up demo ads with special pricing and limited reach on business pages. The ad is usually based on photos, posts, and links you have put on your wall. The targeted distance is 100 to 150 people in your physical area or people with similar interests for around $5.00. The ad appears on the targeted person's timeline, and hopefully, they click to find out about the great food you serve and where you are located. Of course, you can make your ad and not use the demo for the same price.

Cross-promote your location, especially if you move around from day to day or week to week. Post something like, "Today from 11-2 our great dogs are at the corner of 5th and Vine, Saturday we will be at Tom's Hardware on Main." Attach a picture of your set up on 5th and Vine or a picture of your best-looking hot dog. Then on Saturday, post more photos with that location and a tagline for the following area.

Encourage guests to post photos of themselves enjoying your food. Offer discounts based on the number of "shares," "likes," or "retweets."

One promotion I use for new sites or seasonal grand openings is to offer a weekly free hot dog when they share my pre-opening Facebook post, that share gets a certain number of likes, AND they purchase a combo meal on opening day. They get a card numbered 1 thru 52 with good till the date of one year after. I sign the card to prevent copying. The post looks something like this:

Pirate Dogs FWB
Sponsored

Pirate Dogs on Main Opening March 3rd!

Get Free Hot Dogs for a year!
Share this post. Get 25 likes. Order a combo opening day. Show us the post and we'll give you a card for one hot dog a week for a year!

👍 Like 💬 Comment ➡ Share

To make this effective and profitable, simply post the rules on your Facebook page that include:

- Only 1 free hot dog redeemed per week.

- No other purchase required.

- Past missed weeks are lost (no saving up punches).

- Ending date of XX/XX/XXXX (one year from opening).

- Lost cards are not replaced.

- Limited to first 30 (or whatever number you feel comfortable with) people showing correct "like" count.

This program sees 90% redemption the first week in practice, dropping to 50 % the third week. By the end of the second month, only 15% are being redeemed consistently. By the six-month mark, only 1 or 2 a week are saved. I see well over half order chips and a drink to compliment the free hot dog.

If you are a great suggestive salesperson, getting 50% to buy something additional like chips, drinks, and deserts means the original opening budget for this event is completely paid and on the profit side. The exposure is something you just can't put a price tag on.

If you have a decent following of your own on social media, make sure you promote your business there with links, and don't be afraid to ask for your friends and family to do the same.

YouTube: You could even start a channel with live feeds showing your daily operation, the lines, the food, and even your banter with guests. Show a special of the week in a video, as you demonstrate how you cook and dress the dog on your cart. Offer a discount to someone that shows they subscribed to you. As you are getting ready to open, take your phone and shoot a short video showing you in front of your cart saying, "Hey, I am open in front of Bob's Hardware on Central Parkway today, and I have a chili dog with your name on it!!"

Post the video on YouTube/Facebook/Twitter/Instagram, and your subscribers/followers get notifications saying you posted a video. That alone is worth it, reminding your guests you exist whether they watch the video or not. Of course, you could monetize the videos.

Just be wary of what you are doing and how you are set up and organized. Many trolls love putting down other people, so a thick skin is required when you post videos. Also, consider if posting live videos that you have someone available to answer comments and questions; otherwise, you look like you are ignoring your fans.

Facebook Live videos are given preference in rankings on Facebook. They will show up higher in a person's feed than a picture post or a word only post. Use this and post a commercial every day you set up. Again, be funny, witty, and charming. Show off your food, location, and invite folks down to see you. Maybe even offer a discount for sharing your video.

Instagram is the hot media right now for food vendors. Pictures do the selling for you. You can influence Instagram and other social media by understanding and then using the "influencers" of your location or city. On Instagram, search for your town or address if you live in a large city. The search will return the nine most popular posts for that area and the most recent posts.

Select a recent mix (because they are active and nearby) and popular posts (they have an audience) and message each one individually. Sincerely compliment their profile, posts, or pictures and offer them a free signature hot dog (today only) and list your business hours.

Set a daily goal of 30 minutes, reaching out to influencers. You will see 1, to possibly seven people, out of ten collecting on the free hot do in practice. Many of those will purchase at least a drink. Dazzle them with your service and make certain the food you serve to them is outstanding in presentation as it will likely be a photograph on their page.

In a week, you contact 100 people, you will get 10 to 30 new guests, and of that group, at least 1 to 7 will post a photo giving your cart more exposure. Long term, you are looking to connect with that local celebrity, politician, or sports figure that will open many more revenue avenues for you. Network with significant others or partners of these folks as often they create the link to the community and are looking to develop relatable human-interest experiences for their spouse or partner.

Remember, image is everything. If there are no guests to serve, you should be near the road waving, pointing to advertising, and just trying to get attention. Ray Kroc, the McDonalds founder, is famous for saying, "If you got time to lean, you got time to clean!" I have used a time or two in my restaurant career.

As a business owner, "If you got time to sit, your business ain't fit!" If you are onsite and sitting down in between orders, you miss opportunities to engage future guests or draw your business's attention. If you are open for 3 hours, you should be busy for 3 hours. Serving guests, cleaning, prepping, marketing, and answering social media; do something to move your business forward. If you need to sit down all the time, remember, call centers are always hiring!

Using Social Media

The most popular social media tool for food truck owners is Facebook. Facebook is another free tool that shares some similar functionality to Twitter. However, there are certain features on Facebook that are perfect for promoting your food truck. Yes, you can post status updates like Twitter, but you are not limited to a number of characters.

But let's take a small phase back before we talk about actually using Facebook for promotion. First of all, you must set up a personal Facebook account. Getting a Facebook account is much like setting up your Twitter account, so I'm not going to go into too much feature about that here. Their website can walk you step-by-step through the signup process. Chances are you by now have a personal Facebook account you use with friends and family. That is great! However, I do not recommend using your account for your business!

Instead, you'll need to set up a fan page strictly for your food truck.

This is usually tied to your personal Facebook account, but they are independent of each other. A fan page should be used for business because it is viewable by the public and can be found directly through a web search.

When you create your fan page, you will be presented with some categories to classify your business. The natural tendency for food truck owners is to select *"Local Business or Place."* While that seems like a perfect fit, I don't recommend that category for food trucks. Instead, choose *"Company, Organization or Institution"* or *"Brand or Product."* Either one of these categories is perfect for mobile food businesses.

While it is true that a food truck is a local business, you don't necessarily have a street address that would be associated with your vehicle or even regular business hours. You'll be in different locations all the time at other times of the day! When you choose "Local Business or Place," Facebook will ask you to fill out address input boxes for this type of information. The address and hours of operation information will show up at the top of your Facebook page near your profile image. The only reason why a mobile food owner would classify their truck as a "Local Business or Place" would be if they also own a catering company or restaurant and have an actual physical address where people can personally visit during business hours.

However, suppose you already have a fan page for your truck, and you earlier set it up as a "Local Business or Place." In that case, you have the ability (as an administrator) to go in and change it to one of the classifications I mentioned above.

First Impressions on Your Facebook Page

When people visit your Facebook page, the first component they will see is your cover photo. Visitors can't miss it because it's the largest image at the top of the screen. It almost covers the whole width of the Facebook window. You want something compelling and unique for this image! This image should shout out what your food truck is all about!

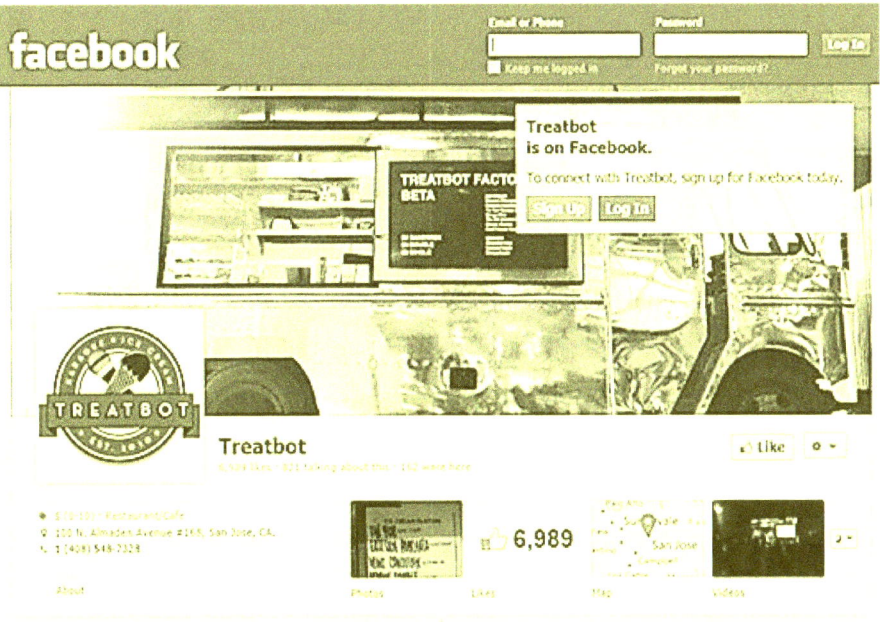

Maybe you could insert a photo of your truck if you have some stunning graphics to show off. Another idea would be to put a clean version of your logo there... but there's a better place for your logo, as we'll explain after. Lastly, you could insert a beautiful image of one of your signature dishes to make people hungry when visiting your page. Just remember that this main image should spark some sort of reaction or make an impression with your visitors.

Technically speaking, this image should be 851x315 pixels at 72dpi (dots per inch) and in JPEG format. The file size should be 100kb or less. If you create an image that does not fit those pixel dimensions, your picture will appear distorted or provide the allotted area in the cover photo window. An image of 851x315 can be created easily in Photoshop. If you don't have Photoshop, a free image editing tool (almost) as good as Photoshop is GIMP. Cover photos can come from your existing Facebook photos, or you can upload a new photo from your computer.

Then, you must upload a profile picture. This is a much smaller image that rests towards the lower left-hand corner of your cover image. Your profile picture denotes your page on other parts of Facebook, advertisements, sponsored stories, and news feeds. You could use almost any image for your profile picture, but I recommend using a logo. This is because Facebook users are going to identify you with this particular image throughout the site. If you already use a Gravatar for your business, I'd recommend using the same appearance as your Gravatar image.

The size of your Facebook profile image needs to be 180x180 pixels. This is the maximum size of the profile image on your main Facebook page. However, this image needs to be scalable down to 32x32 pixels! Why 32x32? This is the size of your profile image when it appears in news feeds. You can check how your image will look by scaling (shrinking) your image in Photoshop or GIMP to see if it is still readable at the smaller 32x32 image size.

Information About Your Business

This part should not be neglected because it will help your Facebook visitors to find out more about your business easily and how they can get in contact with you. I've seen numerous food truck Facebook pages where the owners only filled out minimal information about their business, and it's frustrating when the data is missing. Keep in mind that many people are going to first learn about you on Facebook, and you must create a good first impression. Here are some of the information boxes you can fill out for your profile:

- Address

- About

- Description

- Mission

- Founded

- Awards

- Products

- Phone

- Email

- Website

If I were to pick the most important fields to elaborate on, I'd choose:

- About

- Description

- Products

There's not much room for the description, so keep it short. You might have to play around with the length of this text for it all to fit under your profile image. But depending on the category you choose, the About text may or may not show up in this spot. If you select "Local Business or Place," then information about your operating hours and location will appear here instead.

Setting Up Your Description

The Description is where you should share complete and detailed information about your mobile food business. You're not doing your business any string-pulling when you neglect these areas. People are on your page because they want to find out more about your company! Then in the Products, you can list out some of your most popular dishes and give a short description so readers can get an idea of what's in these menu items.

Instagram

Instagram is based on images, and some food trucks have put it to great use! One of the great advantages about Instagram as a marketing tool is that it allows you to advertise your location to people. This makes it natural for food trucks, since they can direct customers to their location once they've hooked them with exciting pictures of their mouthwatering food. Hashtags are also prominent on it, so be sure to include your business hashtag on everything and you can also pay to publicize your posts.

Twitter

Twitter is a social community that can help build brand awareness and reinforce your connection to a wide audience.

Not only does it allow you to share basic information like your locations and menus, but it also gives you the ability to engage customers with mentions, replies, and retweets.

Twitter is a free marketing tool easy to learn and takes only a few minutes a day to use. Getting followers can take time, but putting forth the effort is well worthwhile! Twitter is based on short messages up to 280 characters long. This is great for promoting events and coupons! You should also use hashtags here on this free platform. Pay to advertise here as well.

LinkedIn

LinkedIn is a social media for professionals. It is good to have a presence here as well, especially if you are marketing to businesses. There are LinkedIn groups you can get into that may help you as you begin your entrepreneurship journey. Paid advertisements are an option, and joining is free like the others.

Chapter 9. Target Market Strategies

Our target marketing strategy will involve identifying a group of customers to direct our mobile food truck products and services. Our approach will be the result of intently listening to and understanding customer needs, representing customers' needs to those responsible for product production and service delivery, and giving customers what they want. In developing our targeted customer messages, we will strive to understand information like: where they work, worship, party, and play, where they buy food and go to school, how they spend their leisure time, and where they volunteer their time. We will use research, surveys, and observation to uncover this wealth of data to get our product details and brand name in front of our customers when they are most receptive to receiving our messaging.

Target Market Worksheet

Item Benefits

Real factors (cost viability, plan, execution, and so forth) or saw factors (picture, prominence, notoriety, and so on) fulfills what a client needs, a favorable position or worth that the item will offer its purchaser.

Products Features

One of the distinguishing characteristics of a product or service helps boost its appeal to potential buyers. An aspect of a product that describes its appearance, its components, and its capabilities.

Typical Features Include Size and Color

The most current ten years have seen an expansion in American's investigations of wellbeing, ethnic, and gourmet nourishments. Regardless of whether this can be ascribed to VIP cooks, travel to far off nations, new wellbeing counts calories, or the expanding availability of once-dark fixings, it appears to be that gourmet and bold palates looking for more beneficial options are staying put.

Numerous inhabitants are presently similarly as refined in their food tastes as our sightseers.

Target Marketing

Target Local Corporations

Numerous huge organizations decide to use both versatile cooking and distributing as food administration choices for their representatives. Rather than battling this reality, we will grasp it, locate a dependable accomplice, and use it as an upper hand.

To market to organizations, we will visit organizations in the zones we intend to work in and request to talk with the director. We will leave a business parcel for future reference. Our business parcel will incorporate a business card, direct mail advertisement, leaflet, a rundown of customers and organizations we have worked for before, and a value sheet. So, they will think of what it will cost to enlist our portable providing food administrations. We will likewise assist the business with a money-saving advantage examination to look at elective foodservice game plans.

Models

Trade shows, workshops, gatherings, representative thankfulness/acknowledgment occasions, leader advancements and retirement parties, Christmas Party, semi-yearly field day, venture achievement achievements, conference lunch get-togethers, and so on.

Target Vending Companies

As a portable food provider, we will work in our grocery store. Distributing organizations, both huge and small, can generally use new frozen treat sources. We intend to give frozen oddities to spreading administrators.

Target Mobile Food Fairs and Festivals

Versatile Food Festivals and Fairs are continually searching for particular merchants to improve their public participation. Variety in frozen pastries will be one route for our organization to champion among other food sellers. We will likewise need to oblige our neighborhood clients' flavors and the necessities of the celebrations and fairs that we join in.

Focus on the Late-Night Entertainment District

We will focus on this part of the city since individuals get ravenous following a late evening to remember. We will focus on our city's diversion area or our neighborhood, famous night spots.

We will acquaint our food truck business with the bar/club proprietor and fabricate our relationship to guarantee they allow us on their property to procure these evening time benefits. We will try to leave our truck sufficiently close to the hot nightspot to tempt benefactors with our food truck's heavenly smells.

Target Food Truck Roundups

We will explore regions where we can incidentally set up close to other food truck administrators to improve our perceivability. We will keep up a decent expert connection with contender food trucks so that we will get welcomed to "their" food truck leave. Food truck proprietors meeting in an isolated area on a reliable day and time will pull in more consideration than a solitary food truck administrator. At a food truck roundup, cafes have more options, so it's simple for visitors to discover menu things to fulfill various tastes. Fruitful food truck proprietors frequently find their business increment when their picked area is a food truck leave since burger joints will test more unique menu things. We will consistently endeavor to pursue occasions that incorporate trucks from non-contending menu classes. We will likewise arrange with trucks that offer comparable menu alternatives to make free timetables, so we both are absent simultaneously.

Target Retail Sponsored Special Events

We will target organizations, for example, vehicle sales centers, that have fantastic day or end of the week occasions and gracefully food. We will visit the vehicle and cruiser vendors and give up a flyer or business card. We will contact the nearby radio broadcasts since they will give a D.J. set for extraordinary occasions and really have the show from experience, and will know about those occasions a long time ahead of time. They might be eager to pass leads on or make a bundle that incorporates a D.J. set and, what's more, food. We will send flyers out via the post office to nearby organizations. We will likewise move toward strip squares because many have trader bunches searching for advancements and different strategies to attract clients to their stores.

Neighborhood beneficent occasions, for example, walk-a-thons and bicycling occasions, draw huge groups. We will offer the coordinators a bit of the gross continues towards their foundation, on the off chance that we can set-up at the occasion.

In June 2010, they gathered Street Food merchants to make an encounter that allowed neighbors to associate with companions and families to reconnect with one another. From that point forward, their occasions have become a Bay Area symbol and quintessential San Franciscan action, known for its extraordinary food and social encounters. They right now work 50+ week by week open occasions all through the San Francisco Bay Area.

Target Beer Festivals

We will target brew celebrations because they frequently search for good quality food to upgrade their specialty lager drinking encounters.

Target Food Truck Parks

These parks offer perpetual areas that are now and again open every minute of every day, seven days per week for food trucks, and can be found in metropolitan and rural regions over the US. These food truck "stops" or "courts," or lasting food truck, regularly include different cooking styles, outside covered seating, kids play zones, parking spots, very much named bathrooms, ATMs, retail sources, and unrecorded music. They have been springing up across the nation. What's more, since trucks have a lot of lower fire up expenses than physical cafés, these parks are a route for new gourmet specialists to set themselves up in the network.

Target Factories, Industrial Complexes, and Office Buildings

We will focus on the laborers at these offices since they can produce consistent recurrent business consistently.

Target Groups Holding Private Events

The new market for distributing truck administrators is private occasions; everything from birthday and commemoration parties, organization picnics, youth baseball games, young men and young ladies clubs excursions.

Target Event Planners

We will advise event and corporate promotion planners of our mobile catering capabilities.

Target Local Concert and Festival Promoters

We will approach concert and festival promoters about the possibility of servicing their attendees at scheduled events.

Target College Administrators

We will ask about the possibility of providing our mobile food truck roundup services on-campus and at major school events, such as graduation ceremonies, community outreach programs, guest lectures, and sports tournaments. Colleges host unique events that feature food trucks and live bands to create a block party experience for students and the community at large.

Target Community Relations Specialists

Community relations specialists are responsible for developing and implementing community outreach programs, including social & community awareness incentives. They work with the organization to create programs that promote the organization's image positively and in a community-oriented way. These specialists typically work for banks, colleges, and large corporations, intending to get these types of businesses more involved in community affairs as a way of giving back to the community and building a sense of goodwill.

Chapter 10. How to Scale Up in Following Years

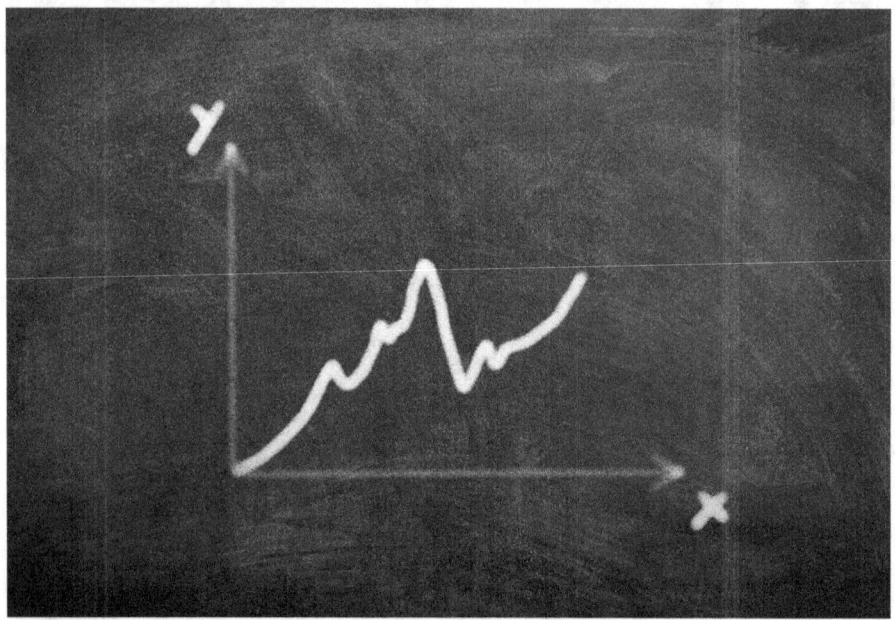

The launchpad is ready to release, and it is time to rev up the engines and stoves of the food truck. Marketing is essential to keep any business running. You should help the company to get noticed so that you can lure in customers. Competitors in the same field of business are never going to rest and make it easier for you. You must advertise and market yourself and your food product efficiently.

Here are some marketing tips that will help you succeed with your food truck business.

Set up Weekly Specials

After the launch, you must gain speed and traffic in business. If a customer likes a specific food item like a Mexican taco, you could have "Taco Tuesdays" to serve the customer's tacos at half the regular price. This will spread the word and will assure you a lot of people.

Be One with the Community

Get close to the community you want to serve. Sponsor for a local sports event or try helping in a charity. Also, find ways to tie up with other business owners in the community.

Hold Contests

People love contests, and they are an excellent idea to promote your food truck business. Promote games through social media and other forms of advertising.

Celebrate Often

You do not need a big reason to celebrate. Opt for smaller holidays and make things exciting and new for the customers. Show the spirit of your celebration through the food you offer.

Have an Inner Circle

Treat your most valuable customers nicely and create an inner circle with them. Offer them discounts and earn their trust by being sweet and pleasant to them.

111

After all this, it is also vital to choose the perfect spot to put up the food truck. Make sure you choose a place where there will be a lot of hungry people. Park your vehicle beside a commercial or industrial space. Also, make it accurate that there are no severe competitors around to spoil your day. When you want to choose a place, find out about the events that might happen regularly. Try to participate in such circumstances and maximize your profit in doing so. Assure that you find out about the ease you can get the licenses to put up your food truck in these events. Do not feel wrong about partnering up. Partner up with a mall or building complex that will allow you to set up a spot on their property.

Feel Free to Market Yourself

Marketing extends beyond the beginning phase, and it is essential to keep the food truck running. Take advantage of digital media and its marketing platforms. Tweet about the places you will put up the stall, connect with Facebook, and maintain a Facebook page to post regular updates. Have a well-planned social media marketing scheme and lure in more customers by showing the merrier sides in dining with you. Also, make sure to deliver the quality and service you have advertised. False advertising can put a hole in the whole process easier.

Think Freely and Do Not Attach Yourself to an Idea

Even if you have found the perfect spot for business and worked well for a long time, there is a likelihood of dwindling sales. Take time to re-plan and think about moving to another new area. Do not be too rigid in the way you think. It is a waste of time, and you might end up losing the business in the process.

Expand on the Revenue Stream

Change with time and try implementing new business ideas. Take gambles and always be on the lookout for new opportunities. Cater to events and festivals to increase the profits you take. Get out of the comfort zone and try new and exciting things. Keep the energy and flow running.

Be Open to Teaming Up

Do not feel wrong about teaming up with other food truck owners out there. You could get a lot out of it because people who eat out of food trucks are most likely to change their trucks often. Pick a crowded place and a friendly food truck owner to club your business with. Cater to that crowded place together and get the best out of that situation. It need not be regularly, but it is good to team up once in a while. People will also love the variety you and your friend in business have to offer.

Keep Networking

Make friends with people who have a strong influence over the place. Drop the prejudice and consider asking other truck owners to get valuable referrals for events and festivals. People might help you, and you might even expand your network. Do not live in your world and miss out on the exposure others have to offer to you.

Make a Good Investment In Your Staff

Ensure you help the staff grow within their positions to stay trustworthy and faithful in the future. It would aid if you treated them with the respect they deserve, and you must acknowledge their excellent work. The means of bringing in and training new staff is not only time-consuming but also costly.

Put a Good Price Tag on Your Food Items

Even if you are new to the business, it is not necessary to offer food for a very cheap rate. If your food is tasty and has outstanding quality, please charge the price that will benefit your system. It is vital to remember that people are ready to pay for the good stuff. Keep your eyes on the quality of the food you serve, and you will see business growth automatically.

These tips and techniques are essential in your path to become a successful food truck owner. Get out there and put out some interesting items on the menu to keep the hungry taste buds on fire. Serve with a bright smile on your face and unconditional love in your heart. There are many people to feed in this world, and it is high time you realize that you can be the change you want to see. Thrive and work hard to serve the tastiest food on wheels and make sure you touch people's lives with what you do.

Work on Your Customer Service Skills

There are two straightforward ways for street food businesses to increase their sales: get new business or increase repeat business.

Repeat business is invaluable and will encourage word of mouth referrals, customer confidence and enhance your reputation. But how do you keep your customers coming back time and time again?

Aside from the food, the customer experience is what will ensure your customers return to buy from you again. Think of a time when you received incredible customer service and then compare it with a time when you received terrible customer service—which one are you most likely to revisit?

The value of making customers happy, treating them well and giving them a 5-star experience cannot be underestimated. It's also incredibly easy and cheap to do! Simple things like remembering to smile, treating everyone equally and going the extra mile for each customer will generate a positive experience and a happy memory for each person that you serve. People are also more likely to discuss negative experiences than positive ones, so try to keep those to a minimum!

Why not consider offering incentives and freebies to loyal customers, too? Try out a customer loyalty scheme, a free hot drink scheme or exclusive extras for those who visit you regularly.

Chapter 11. Customer Reward Program

Getting new customers is the way you grow your business. It's no wonder that companies exert a lot of time and money to bring in new customers. Studies have revealed that it costs 5 to 10 times more to acquire a new customer than selling to a loyal existing customer.

There's also research that demonstrates that existing customers spend 67% more than new customers. So you can see that keeping customers coming back is extremely beneficial to your food truck business. The mobile food industry is very competitive, so you need to attract and retain customers to buy from you and not your competitors.

So what can you do to keep your customers coming back and spending their money with you? The answer is with a customer loyalty program. A good portion of businesses has implemented some customer loyalty or rewards program to entice customers to come back and buy.

American Airlines was a few of the first to implement a customer loyalty program on a large scale and was the first widely accepted program in the United States. The idea was to give their passengers something special for flying with them. This was the first frequent flyer program that allowed passengers to accrue miles to use on future flights as long as they continued to fly on American Airlines. Today, regular flyer programs are commonplace in the airline industry.

Loyalty programs work the best with businesses that serve repeat customers. Restaurants and food trucks fall into that category. If you have amazing food and great customer service, you will get repeat customers. To keep them coming back, reward them for their continued patronage. How many times have you visited a restaurant to get that 11th sandwich for free?

Effective Loyalty Programs

You've probably seen a loyalty program in many businesses you've visited. But a loyalty program is simply a rewards program that companies offer to customers that make frequent purchases. This loyalty program rewards customers who keep coming back with special offers, gifts, free merchandise, coupons, and more!

While loyalty programs seem like it's simple to implement, let me throw out the following facts.

A recent study has shown that a given household typically has memberships to 29 loyalty programs. However, only 12 out of all those who have signed up are engaged. That means many companies and spending a lot of time and money on rewards programs but seeing very little to no benefit from them. The key is to offer value to your customers for being a part of your loyalty program. How do you increase your ability to make loyalty programs more effective for your food truck business?

Loyalty Program Features

Many companies offer loyalty programs, and the choices can be overwhelming. Some are simple, while others are feature-rich and advanced. It's important to pick the one you think will work with your food truck business for the long term. However, you can never tell if these loyalty programs will close shop or acquire a larger rewards program. But you can't allow that fear to stop you from implementing a loyalty program.

I will give you some ideas and suggestions when searching for a loyalty program that is right for you. Use this as a guide to be better informed before you implement a system for your food truck. It is not uncommon to switch programs if you find that it is not working for you over time. Here are some suggestions and features to consider.

Simple Point Systems

One of the most common and oldest loyalty program systems is the point system. Customers that visit your food truck frequently can accrue points that can be redeemed for rewards once they've reached the threshold you've set. They can receive a discount, free items or even special treatment and more!

You've seen these before, and can come in many forms. Some are simple punch cards, while others use magnetic cards and a database to track points. The point system should be simple to understand. Don't over-complicate this! The term points can refer to various tracking methods. For example:

- Buy ten sandwiches get the 11th free

- Spend $50 get your after dish free

The point system encourages frequent short-term purchases that keep customers returning, accruing points, and eventually getting rewarded for their continued visits to your food truck. You can assign points by the number of items or by the dollar amount spent.

Tier System

There is a tricky balance between a loyalty program and offering attainable and desirable rewards. You must not create a huge process for customers to reach reward thresholds. That will turn off your customers, and your loyalty system becomes ineffective. One way to breach this problem is to use a tier system.

With a tier system, you can offer a reward for initially joining your loyalty program. This encourages sign-ups. Then you can bring back returning customers by increasing the value of the prizes you offer in different tiers. Each tier is made more attractive by offering higher value or better tips as they move up the ladder. This can help customers remember your loyalty program because it encourages decreasing the time it takes to redeem their rewards. If the time between payouts for the compensation is too long, customers will forget or ignore the loyalty program. The biggest disparity between a points system and a tier system is that customers receive their short-term rewards.

So with your food truck business, you can offer a free appetizer or drink for the initial sign-up to your loyalty program. After that, you can provide larger and larger rewards such as complimentary appetizers when they reach the following tier and then offer something else in subsequent stories.

How to Measure Effectiveness

Just because you've implemented your loyalty program, it doesn't mean you're done! You need to be able to measure the success of your efforts. The goal of your loyalty program is to increase your customer's satisfaction and keep them coming back.

You will most likely be using a rewards program with an online database in today's business world. These systems offer excellent tracking and analytics. A punch card system can work, but it will be much more difficult to evaluate its effectiveness.

Customer Retention Rate

When evaluating your analytics, you should first look at your Customer Retention Rate. This is a measurement of how long your customers continue to buy from you. If your loyalty program is successful, this number should increase over time as you continue to add people to your schedule. Studies have shown that even a 5% increase in customer retention can translate to a 25% to 100% increase in your company's profits.

Negative Churn

You may or may not have heard the term churn. But churn is the rate at which your customers stop doing business with you. When I say negative churn, it indicates the status at which customers increase spending with you. Negative churn helps to balance out the natural occurrence where customers leave your business.

Net Promoter Score

The net promoter score is grounded on customer satisfaction and how likely they recommend your business to others. This is usually on a scale of 1 to 10, with ten being the highest. The net promoter score is designed by taking the percentage of detractors (people who wouldn't promote your business) and subtracting it from the number of promoters (people who would recommend your company).

The fewer detractors you have, the better. You can consider a net promoter score of 70% and a higher good number, and having a great loyalty program can help you reach that number. To get the satisfaction rating, you will have to send out surveys to customers. These are usually based online and can be sent as notifications via your chosen loyalty program.

When to Implement a Loyalty Program?

Loyalty programs can be implemented at any time during your business. For some older enterprises, they've been doing business for years before starting a loyalty program. That could be because reliable systems weren't available when they started, and now they realize the benefits of having it.

Others start a loyalty program from the beginning or early on. But here's a suggestion. If you haven't launched your food truck yet, get on board with a loyalty company that fits your business. Have it in place before you launch. When you launch your vehicle, you can start customers on your loyalty program right from the start. Hold a special event when you launch and make sure you let customers know about the program.

If you cater to events, this is also a great place to gather multiple signups in one location. When you're at a catering event, guests have more time to spend with you and your business. Keep in mind

122

any circumstances where you have to opportunity to sell your loyalty program.

I can't go into detail about all the loyalty programs available to businesses, but I can list some of them, so you have a good starting point to research the best one for your food truck business. I can't choose one for you but the information.

Here is a short list to get you started. These companies can come and go so that some of them may or may not be in business anymore by the time you read this.

- Belly
- Square
- LevelUp
- FiveStars
- Wali
- Perka
- SpotOn
- PunchCard
- SpendGo
- Swipley
- FourSquare

Most if not all the rewards systems listed above use mobile apps and digital tracking to make it easy for your customers to path their reward status. This helps customers know when they are close to receiving a reward and could entice them to come back for a visit.

Choosing Rewards for Customers

The kind of rewards offered to customers varies depending on the type of business. But there are some general rules to follow and increase the chances of a positive reward experience for your customers. Experts advise expanding your thinking from only offering discounts on your goods. That's because the deals don't have a long-lasting impact on customer's impressions. Rewards that have physical items are received and remembered much better than a plain discount. Luckily, in the food truck industry, we can talk straight to customer's stomachs!

A good way to tailor your rewards program is to imitate larger successful programs from related companies and offering something unique. You can research brick-and-mortar restaurants, bakeries, ice cream shops, food trucks, and more to see what they are doing.

It's a well-known fact that loyalty programs are a very effective marketing tool. When successfully implemented, they can help increase profits and keep customers coming back for more. Loyalty programs can also help boost your brand awareness and, ultimately, your reputation. If you haven't done so, start researching the different loyalty programs available and plan out how you would implement them into your business. You don't want to be missing out on an excellent marketing opportunity that can result in a lot of positive advantages for your food truck!

Chapter 12. Hiring Employees

With food trucks, you will quickly notice that there is often much more work than just two people can perform. When hiring employees, it's best to start with one additional set of helping hands at a time, depending on your schedule.

Knowledge is the most important aspect when hiring an employee. You must be a knowledgeable employer to find the ideal employee. You'll need to follow procedures from the Small Business Administration and learn about tax withholdings, wages, and insurance when it comes to your employees.

Additional research about hiring is important to ensure all of your tactics meet those roles defined by the government. Only after completing all guidelines, should you consider hiring outside help.

When hiring, define roles on paper to make sure everyone understands their specific responsibilities, including you. Decide if you are going to be working alongside your customers or working directly in the kitchen. This will help define an employee's skill set.

Finally, it's important to understand the mobile cuisine business culture. Certain values, traditions, and practices must be met and followed. Define the type of culture and environment you hope to operate and find employees that share your vision to succeed.

Finding the Right Kind of Help

Because a handful of individuals only operates food trucks, they must understand their role individually while also working as a team. Staffing a food truck depends on some factors, with each worker having specific, defined roles.

The extent of your food truck and the flow of customers will dictate how many employees are needed. Workers also need room to work comfortably to be the most efficient during their job.

You should have a good grasp of the amount of food that needs to be prepared when deciding how many employees to hire. No matter how much work you think you can do alone, there will always be a time when you'll need additional help.

Food trucks require front and back house employment, much like a restaurant. Front of house (FoH) handles customer service and contact while back of the house (BoH) performs operational tasks such as cleaning, cooking, and possibly bookkeeping, depending on what lessons you need to be done.

Front of house employees is in charge of taking orders, preparing checks, and accepting payments. Still, these front workers must also understand the back of housework to inform the customers about ingredients, etc.

The chef usually runs the Back of the house and takes responsibility for everything inside of the food truck, including the service flow, training, and hiring in most cases. The chef is also responsible for culinary certifications, daily menus, buying supplies and ingredients, plus equipment maintenance.

For larger trucks, there are also kitchen workers who are in charge of prepping and weighing ingredients. These workers can also peel, clean, or slice when needed and make salads or other sides that do not require cooking. However, a lot of this work can be performed ahead of time in a commissary or commercial kitchen.

Managing Your Employees

While some management positions require employees and employers to work in more isolated quarters, many food truck operators may feel closer to their workers due to the tight quarters within a food truck.

With that in mind, there are still basic practices to follow to keep workers enthusiastic about their jobs. Start by remembering to always provide constructive, positive feedback to employees working for you. Feedback is the foundation of great management.

Respect each employee as an individual, never negatively grouping them. Make sure each person feels respected during their job, despite their roles or responsibilities. Doing so will help everyone go the extra mile during work hours.

Perhaps the most important step is to provide adequate training to all employees. This not only creates confidence, but it makes sure everyone is working safely and efficiently. Consider enrolling in leadership training to develop closer relationships in business.

Disciplining Employees

The act of firing an employee can be as daunting on you as the individual you're letting go of. According to The Wall Street Journal, firing an employee is one of the three most stressful tasks of any company president or boss. Don't feel alone in this if you have never been in this situation. Even high-powered executives have trouble with this.

Before getting to the point of firing an employee, it is first important to make sure that everyone knows there are clear rules to be followed by all employees, to define the line between an adequate employee and those prone to disciplinary measures.

The methods in which rules are established and enforced are truly what make an operation run methodically. It is then easier to see any missing links in the chain, which can therefore be dealt with accordingly.

The rules you set should always be reasonable, and employees should be determined to adhere to the regulations before actual employment. In addition to delivering the regulations, any potential consequences should also be conveyed to the employee right from the beginning.

If an employee breaks one of the stated rules, disciplinary action may be in order. First, develop an employee warning system by calmly reminding them of the law or standard that has been broken.

If the issue persists, consider giving a more stern warning, possibly including a written document of notice. If the problem still persists, it may be time to consider a probationary period, docking the worker from shifts for a certain period.

All warnings—written or verbal—should be presented calmly, taking the time to answer any questions while offering additional assistance to conduct the work as it should be performed. Either way, keep track of warnings in an employee file.

With warnings, make sure these are given in a way to be taken seriously. If the issue deserves a sign, treat it with respect, in a serious manner.

Termination should be the last step. Ensure the employee in question has been presented the facts and that multiple resolution measures have been attempted before actually firing them.

When a looming termination seems unavoidable, make sure the person in question is truly at fault for the situation before taking that final action.

Importance of Employee Feedback

Perhaps one of the most effective ways for managers to develop efficient employees is to give performance feedback—both positive and negative. Constructive feedback fixes small problems, but it creates a type of career development for the individual.

Employee feedback provides satisfaction, retention, and motivation and it should be given often, both spontaneous when an action occurs and sometimes on a schedule.

If you don't provide employee feedback, you can miss a golden opportunity to shape further and develop your employees. Rather than waiting to tell an individual, their performance has been lacking after six months, take the time to fix the problems right from the beginning.

Remember, providing feedback doesn't have to be presented as a disciplinary task. Instead, be constructive, open a conversation with the employee, and absorb their interests to create positive behaviors and future incentives to help the entire group achieve.

Handling the Competition

The food truck business is highly competitive, despite your cooking skills or locations. With so many trucks already existing, standing out can be difficult. Generally, taking a competitive edge requires learning the demographics, adopting successful strategies, and working hard.

With restaurants, many owners will try to find an area where no competitors can be found. However, in the food truck business, there will always be a little fight to be had, so the best bet is to create a niche within a niche—providing affordable, specialty items.

Among the competition, there are direct and indirect competitors. Direct competitors offer the same primary services as if there were two pizza trucks in the area. On the other hand, indirect competitors provide similar services as a wider range of products, such as another food truck that offers a side that may be your main dish.

Rather than becoming overwhelmed, consider monitoring all of your competition regularly to learn behaviors and anticipate potential moves. Once the competition has been properly analyzed, you can then plan your battle strategies.

Start by digging in with social media and reporting on local food trucks. If another car is in the paper, find out how this happened— whether they know someone in the business or were simply brought in by word-of-mouth.

Within the realms of social media, find out what others are saying about your competitors, taking advice and criticism to adapt your own business. Afterward, speak to your customers in a friendly manner to find out your strengths.

Speaking to customers is perhaps the most efficient manner to learn about the competition. Find out why they are buying food from your truck and take any suggestions to improve sales. See what they dislike and make modifications if it makes sense.

Attending related conferences and joining industry associations are a good idea to keep tabs on what's going on in the industry. These methods will put you ahead of the curve, making you the most knowledgeable individual on the market.

Another strategy is to speak with your suppliers to learn more about your competitor's volume. While you may not find this information directly from another food truck, you could get suppliers to divulge critical information you could never get from your competitors.

Finally, conduct a survey. Find a way to get information from your customers without bugging them. For example, consider reaching out on social media or give away products like shirts or hats that feature your logo in exchange for information.

Chapter 13. Food Truck Troubleshooting

The Mobile Food Truck will be run as a group, with every worker having an important influence on the business' prosperity or disappointment. Workers will be given whatever apparatuses and preparing are considered significant to do their tasks. An accentuation on cycle improvement will be imparted in each of the "colleagues" by offering rewards or extraordinary advantages. Partners will be compensated for both fiscally and non-financially tasks all around finished. Powerful correspondence will be pushed in business. This will eliminate errors and miscommunications among clients, representatives, and administrators. Week after week, meetings should be held to examine the week by week timetable and report last week's happenings. Colleagues will be permitted to add contributions to these meetings in proposals, remarks, and objections. Colleagues will have characterized errands; however, they are available to do whatever demands outside of their set rules should be made to carry the training.

In any case, making progress in the food truck world is significantly more confounded than is frequently seen. Like cafés, food trucks have an exceptionally high disappointment rate, with 60% going under within three years of opening.

Various factors can add to food truck frustration. Anyway, essential clarification is likely distorted. People thinking with their spirits closed can undoubtedly reach their targets by opening a food truck and dismissing various huge nuances. Visionaries acknowledge that commitment to fantastic food, getting resources to buy a vehicle, and covering overhead will prepare to advance.

Since starting a food truck is more reasonable than various free endeavors, it doesn't mean opening one is a guaranteed way to achieve autonomy from a futile daily existence. Breaking into the food truck world requires difficult work, a solid financial course of action, and a patient, productive interest.

Causes Food Trucks Go Down and How to Prevent Them

To see additionally concerning why food trucks crash and burn, it is ideal to look at what business zones can over-burden it. The territories underneath talk about different reasons that food trucks ordinarily miss the mark, and all fall under the umbrella of twisting. With accurate, reasonable, and point by point orchestrating, the sum of the going with episodes can be avoided.

Nonattendance of Business and Financial Knowledge

A food truck is, paying little heed to whatever else, a business. Similarly to any company, the appropriate methodology should give a solid foundation to the association. It may be anything other than hard to get stirred up in organizing imaginative menu items. Anyway, the food isn't the fundamental portion requiring comprehensive idea preceding opening a food truck.

Without a predefined arrangement of costs, operational cycles, promoting and stamping plans, and assessment into industry-express issues, any food truck may, without a doubt, miss the mark.

Nuances covering the fundamental licenses, awards, and security to guarantee food truck—unequivocal laws and rules are sometimes disregarded by people needing to open food trucks. Each state, district, and city has its laws for food trucks, and not having the correct licenses and permits can provoke heavy fines.

Obstruction with ever-changing prosperity office standards can incite issues. Insurance, moreover, requires prior organizing. A couple of individuals wanting to start a food truck barely care about the cost of having insurance covering their business, similarly to their real truck.

Significant expenses are a regular clarification of food trucks crash and burn. Not only are particular costs a portion of the time barely cared about, yet some can in like manner be ignored totally. Beginning an adaptable business can pass on various unforeseen costs like the truck and stuff upkeep, fuel, and leaving tickets.

A fair assessment concerning the most awful that could happen is fundamental when starting a food truck. Only assembling a money related game plan for a set improvement course of occasions may not be convincing. Various food truck owners end up spending more money on their business than they had foreseen from the start. They suffer disproportionate number of unwanted stuns that they cannot cover.

Another factor in food truck disillusionment is the absence of authentic appreciation of accounting. Definitely evaluating and fittingly following expenses and advantages is crucial to having a productive movement, especially in an industry with minimal general incomes.

Any food truck owner must deal with payment and know where each dollar is being spent. They must moreover ensure that each dollar is being spent in the best way possible. Food trucks can bomb in light of not recommended stock organization and slandered food costs.

Without coordinating explicitly how capital will be spent and why, the future may not show astonishing for a business. Some food truck proprietors devise an approach to manage, improve, and get the additional preferred position by offering kinds of help, for example, cooking.

Absence of Management and People Skills

The culinary limit isn't the essential wellness basic to run a profitable food truck. The capacity to administer set up and talk with individuals is central. A dreadful association can annihilate any business. Different individuals who open food trucks can do a gigantic portion of the work themselves yet can't advise others on the ideal approach to manage each commitment.

Without a clear idea worked inside and out, informational cycles, plans, and instructional flyers related to the basic method, a food truck won't be able to run for long. Starting with the basic enrolled worker, staff individuals need to keep up the business relatively as the proprietor does.

Obviously, without complete responsibility from the proprietor, a food truck can fizzle. A food truck proprietor should be dependably present at their foundation to guarantee their vision is being executed unequivocally. The possibility of their thing and association is up to their guidelines. Right, when a proprietor isn't around to ensure work is being done as they might want, food quality can endure, and clients can be lost.

Food truck proprietors must not just have the decision to allow their courses of action to other people. At any rate, they should additionally have the choice to look at others. Looking at subject matter experts and their considerations regarding making a business run considerably more satisfactorily, may prompt momentous actions, yet not doing so won't bring thwarted expectation.

In any case, if a proprietor doesn't look at issues representatives may have concerning the way where they are overseen or surveyed, it could incite a disappointed and angry staff passing their emotions onto clients as horrendous assistance or to a high turnover rate that makes it hard to prepare staff individuals to offer great service and food.

What the client needs to state is impressively more enormous. Food trucks can bomb when their proprietors have made plans to think that they can't orchestrate great changes. If a food truck is battling, its proprietor must decide to dissect and evaluate why and perhaps scrap some menu things that were huge for the concept they chose to begin the food truck in any case.

Steadily enduring that their examinations are the best insights and that clients will, as time goes on, concur, can bring a food truck proprietor superfluous issues and conceivably cost them the business.

Chapter 14. Food Safety and Food Poisoning

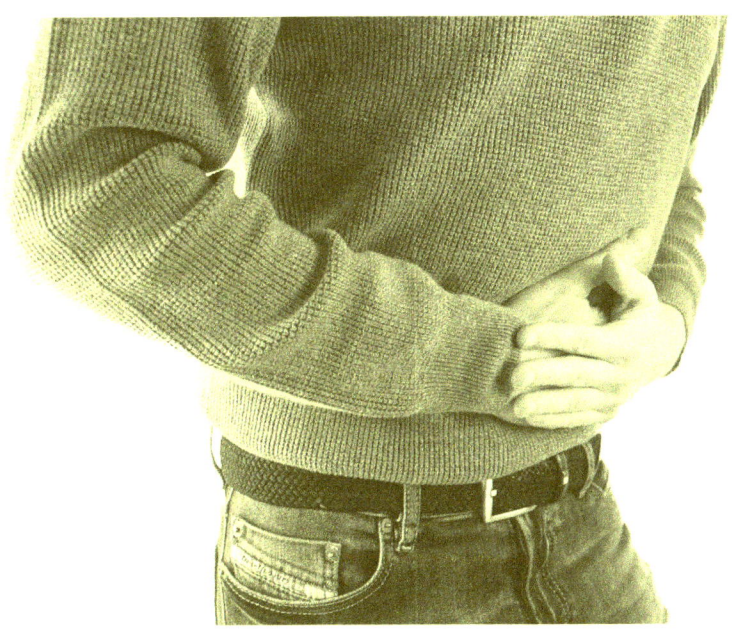

What is food poisoning? It is an acute illness, generally sudden, realized by eating contaminated or noxious food. Food poisoning symptoms vary with the source of contamination. Most types of food poisoning cause one or more of the following signs and symptoms:

1. Nausea – a queasy feeling as though you were going to be sick

2. Sickness – heaving

3. Pain in the bowl – holding torments in the area of the stomach

4. Diarrhea

5. Fever

The essential driver of food contamination are:

- Bacteria – the commonest
- Viruses – which are more modest than microscopic organisms
- Chemicals – Insecticides and weed-executioners
- Metals – lead pipes, copper dish
- Harmful plants – toadstools, red kidney beans (deficiently cooked)

Microbes are the most widely recognized sort of food contamination; along these lines, we must get some answers concerning them.

Microbes are unassuming bugs that live recognizable for what it's worth, in water, in soil, on and in individuals, in and on food. A few microbes cause disease. They are called PATHOGENIC microbes. A few microorganisms cause food to rot. They are called SPOILAGE microorganisms.

Warmth

They love an internal heat level of 73°C (163°F) yet can happily develop at 15 degrees C (59F). They become most promptly somewhere in the range of 5°C (41°F) and 63°C (146°F). This is known as the DANGER ZONE

Time

Each bacterium creates by separating fifty-fifty. Taking everything into account, at standard spans.

Dampness

They need water, and most foods have enough water or sogginess to permit the microorganisms to prosper.

A few microorganisms can shape a hard-protective case around themselves; this is known as a SPORE. This happens when the 'going gets remarkable' when it gets nonsensically hot or pointlessly dry. This way, they can suffer incredibly hot or cold temperatures and can even be accessible in dried foods. When the right conditions (5-63°C) return, the spore rises out of its cautious bundling, creating food pollution as tiny life forms once more.

Microscopic Life Forms and Food Poisoning

We have explained that microorganisms' presence is one of the most broadly perceived explanations behind food pollution—the presence of destructive manufactured mixes can correspondingly cause food defilement. There are a couple of conceivably unsafe engineered substances present in food. For example, potatoes that have turned green contain Solanine's hazardous substance, which is essentially unstable when eaten in excess.

- Rhubarb contains Oxalic Acid—the wholes present in the stems which are reliably cooked are respectably harmless to

141

people. Yet, the higher concentration in the leaves makes them outstandingly dangerous to eat.

- A poison is a destructive substance that might be conveyed by processing a plant or animal, especially certain tiny living beings. Dangerous food pollution is essentially achieved by Staphylococci in the UK and even more sometimes in this country, Clostridium Botulinum.

Nourishments most ordinarily impacted by Staphylococci are:

- Meat pies
- Sliced Meats
- Pies with sauce
- Synthetic cream
- Ice-cream

50-60% of people pass on Staphylococci in their noses and throats and are accessible in nasal releases following an infection. Staphylococci are likewise present in skin wounds and infections and discover their way into foods using the hands of a spoiled food handler, consequently, the necessity of keeping all injuries and skin conditions covered. Notwithstanding how staphylococci are quickly crushed through careful cooking or warming, the toxic substance they produce is consistently impressively safer when warm and may require a higher temperature or longer cooking time for its pummeling.

Foods most normally affected by Clostridium botulinum are:

Inadequately arranged canned meat, vegetables, and fish.

During the business canning measure, each care is taken to ensure that each piece of the food is warmed to an adequately high temperature to ensure pulverization of any Clostridium botulinum spores that might be accessible.

- *Yeasts and Molds* – little living things, some of which are alluring in food and add to its characteristics. For example, the development of cheddar, bread maturing, etc. They are essential plants that seem like hairs on food. To be created, they require warmth, sogginess, and air. They are killed by heat and light. Molds can develop where there is too little soddenness for yeasts and minute life forms to create. Yeasts are single-celled plants or creatures greater than bacteria produced on foods containing sogginess and sugar. Foods having somewhat sugar levels and a broad extent of fluid, for instance, juices and syrups, are liable to age considering yeasts. Yeasts are crushed by heat.

- *Contamination* – minute particles imparted by food, which may cause infection, for example, Hepatitis A (jaundice). As opposed to microorganisms, contaminations can't add or fill in food.

- *Protozoa* – single-celled day-by-day schedule structures with water involvement and are subject to certifiable disorders, for instance, wild fever, generally spread by polluted mosquitoes and looseness of the bowels. These food-borne sicknesses are, by and large, gotten abroad.

- *Escherichia Coli* – E. Coli is a regular piece of the assimilation plots of man and animals. It is found in human excreta and rough meat.

- *Salmonella* – is accessible in the stomach related organs of animals and individuals. It impacts poultry, meat, eggs, and shellfish.

Control of Bacteria

There are three strategies for controlling minute living beings:

1. Shield food from microorganisms detectable all around by keeping it covered. Use separate sheets and cutting edges for cooked and uncooked foods to prevent cross-pollution. Use different closed containers for explicit material. For example, red for meat, blue for fish, yellow for poultry, etc. Store cooked and uncooked foods adequately. Wash your hands frequently.

2. Take the necessary steps to avoid keeping foods in the danger zone of someplace in the scope of 5°C and 63°C (41-145°F) for more time than should be normal.

3. To wipe out microorganisms, subject them to a temperature of 77°C (171°F) for 30 seconds or a higher temperature for less time. Certain microorganisms structure into spores and

144

can withstand higher temperatures for more widened periods. Certain artificial materials in similar way kill tiny creatures and can be used for cleaning stuff and utensils.

The basic food neatness rules of criticalness to the cook are Food Safety (General Food Hygiene) Regulations 1995 and Food Safety (Temperature Control) Regulations 1995. These executed the EC Food Hygiene request (93/43 EEC). They replaced a couple of interesting rules, including the Food Safety (General) Regulations of 1970. The 1995 Regulations are indistinguishable in various respects to earlier laws. Regardless of the Health and Safety authorization, these rules place a strong highlight on owners and heads to perceive the security dangers and design and execute reasonable structures to hinder pollution.

These structures and frameworks are covered by *Hazard Analysis Critical Control Points (HACCP)* or possibly Assured Safe Catering. The rules place two general requirements on owners of food associations to ensure that all food managing exercises are done neatly and shown by the 'Rules of Hygiene.'

What's more, there is a responsibility on any food controller who may be experiencing or conveying an infection which could be communicated through food, to report this to the business who may be obliged to forestall the individual worried from managing food. Cooking foundations have a general obligation to oversee and teach and prepare sanitation and cleanliness comparable with their representatives' duties. Insights concerning how much exercise is required are not determined in the guidelines. Notwithstanding,

145

HMSO Industry Guide to Catering gives direction on preparing, which can be considered a prevailing norm to follow enactment.

Prevention of Food Poisoning

Practically all food poisoning can be prevented by:

- Complying with the rules of hygiene.
- Ensuring that high standards of cleanliness are applied to premises and equipment.
- Preventing accidents.
- Keeping high standards of personal hygiene.
- Keeping up great working conditions.
- Keeping up equipment in decent shape and clean condition.
- Using separate equipment and knives for cooked and uncooked foods.
- Keeping an ample arrangement of cleaning facilities and equipment.
- Putting away foods at the correct temperature.
- Reheating foods safely.
- Cooling quickly of foods before storage.
- Protecting of foods from vermin and insects.
- Hygienic cleaning up procedures.

This has been only a brief overview of food safety. If you are in the catering trade or are preparing yourself to become a cook or chef, you must learn everything to think about the subject. The simultaneous connections should help to fill the holes.

Chapter 15. Understanding Important Laws And Regulations

Taking your food truck out on the road is exciting, but before you begin preparing and selling food, you need to understand the important laws and regulations surrounding food trucks. You need to have the proper licenses, insurance for your business, and you will need to follow important health and safety guidelines. Certain taxes will need to be paid as well. Dealing with all the laws, licenses, and regulations can be one of the most frustrating parts of starting your street food business, but with some help, you will get through this step and on to indulge in your passion for food.

Taxes

Since you are self-employed, you will have certain taxes you need to pay. Tax law requires you to register with HM Revenue and Customs within the first three months of being self-employed. Self-employed individuals are responsible for taking care of their taxes and their National Insurance contributions. Each year, you will be required to fill in a tax return. If you are unsure of what you need to do to file taxes when you are self-employed, you can call the HMRC helpline or talk to a local tax office.

Food Licenses And Registration

To begin operating your street food business, you will need to have the right food licenses and registration. Food businesses are required to have the necessary registration with their local council before starting to trade. You will need to register your street food business with the local council in the area where you store your vehicle at least 28 days before opening your new business. Do not make the mistake of registering where you operate—make sure you register with the local council in the area where your vehicle is stored since registrations are checked regularly.

Suppose you are running a mobile food premise. In that case, you are also required to have a valid vehicle excise license (which is a road tax), an insurance certificate for your vehicle, and a certificate of roadworthiness for your car. People that will come in contact with food also have to have appropriate training. The training level required will depend on the particular job. It is also possible that you will need some specific licenses, depending on your business. For example, if you sell alcohol, you will need support for liquor and entertainment. This license is also required if you plan to sell beverages or food between 11 pm and 5 am.

Insurance

To legally run your street food business, you need to be properly insured as well. Whether you are using a trailer or a van for your business, you need good insurance. Several insurance options are available to you when you start looking for one.

- *Product Liability Insurance* – This insurance is a great idea if you will run a street food business in the UK. This will help keep your business protected from claims made against your company if beverages or drinks are accidentally served or cause food poisoning. Medical expenses will be taken care of for those affected if the request is justified.

- *Public Liability Insurance* – This type of insurance helps to protect your business from claims the public may make against you due to accidental injury or accidental property damage that occurs at the hands of your street food business.

- *Employers' Liability Insurance* – If you hire employees, you must legally carry employers' liability insurance. If a member of your staff is made ill or injured accidentally on the job, this insurance covers damage pay-outs and legal fees you may face. In a hot kitchen, accidents can quickly occur, so this insurance is important.

- *Catering Van Insurance* – Not only do you need insurance for your business, but your van must legally be insured as well. Many companies offer catering van insurance, with various levels of cover available. Of course, while different policies can offer many additional features, the following are a few important features you may want to consider.

No Claims Bonus – If you already have a no claims bonus on your private vehicle policy, insurance companies may be willing to offer you a no claims bonus on your catering van policy as well. Ask your insurance company about this feature before choosing your insurance.

Comprehensive Cover – If something happens to your van, your business could quickly go under. This means you should probably consider a comprehensive cover for your vehicle. Ask about new for old cover as well, which means that if your van is a total loss, you will receive a pay-out that considers what you will have to spend to get a new truck for your street food business.

Road Assistance and Towing – You cannot afford to be left high and dry if you break down. When purchasing the insurance for your van, look for a policy that offers roadside assistance and towing.

Breakdown cover can be a great option, which can help you recover the loss you experience if a breakdown occurs.

Contents Insurance – A general insurance plan for your van only covers the vehicle. Since you probably will be spending a large amount of money on equipment in your van, having contents insurance is a great idea. This way, you get coverage for your fryers, stoves, fridges, and other equipment you have in your food truck.

Health and Safety

Certain health and safety regulations must be followed. If your food truck does not follow these regulations for mobile food businesses, it could affect your right to trade, which your local council enforced and administered. You may have to undergo food safety inspections at regular intervals. Any waste from your mobile business must be disposed of as trade waste, meaning that you cannot dispose of it as domestic waste.

Cross-contamination is one of the big risks that mobile catering businesses face. To avoid this, certain health and safety guidelines must be followed. Some of those guidelines include the following:

- Cleaning out sinks after raw foods or vegetables are washed or prepared in them;
- Avoid touching food with your hands;
- Chopping boards and food prep areas must be cleaned and disinfected;
- Cooked food and raw foods must be kept separate;

- Food must never be stored on the ground and should be at least 45 cm above the ground;
- Equipment needs to be disinfected and cleaned after every use.

Your food truck must also follow certain temperature control and storage regulations. These guidelines are important because it helps to avoid food poisoning. Some of the policies you should be tracking include:

- Cooked food needs to reach 75°C (167°F) at its core;
- Hot food should be kept at a minimum of 63C (146°F);
- Food should be immediately prepared before serving;
- High-risk foods like dairy and meat products should be kept cold at 8°C (46°F) or below;
- Thermometers should be used to check the temperature of cooked foods;
- When storing food in the refrigerator, it should be covered.

Of course, these are just a few of the health and safety guidelines and regulations that must be followed. To learn more about your area's food safety requirements, contact your local councils' Food, Healthy & Safety division for more information.

Chapter 16. Nine Best Locations For Your Food Truck Business

B efore committing to starting up a food truck, you must sure that your idea will stand out against the existing market. Start by researching your city for the following:

- Existing food truck businesses and concepts
- Existing restaurant concepts
- The average demographic of the population
- Space where food trucks can stop and sell their products
- Busy street times where commuters can become customers

Be sure to find out if there is a demand in your city for the food truck concept you'll be interested in presenting. We offer here nine best locations for your food truck business.

1. Unique Events

On the off chance that you remain in a socially dynamic city, you should exploit this. Keep awake-to-date on all the get-togethers that occur in your general vicinity, for example, celebrations and shows, and inquire on which of these events are available to food trucks.

Become more acquainted with the vital contacts at the guest's dresser and the coordinators at all the famous occasions that occur during the year in your general vicinity. You will get more solicitations to partake in these occasions if you begin growing great connections directly from the beginning.

Uncommon occasions can be an entirely beneficial spot to leave your food truck since it will give you admittance to the visitors that participate to the occasions, which implies that you don't have to do much in the method of advancement. Be watching out for yearly occasions and attempt to fabricate decent compatibility with the occasion's coordinators so you will consistently be welcomed.

It would be best if you observed that the occasion might be dropped prompting a deficiency of cash on your part in case of an unexpected terrible climate. Also, if the crowd at the occasion doesn't coordinate your client profile, you may wind up not making a ton of deals even though there are a ton of visitors present at the party. For example, hamburgers and French fries probably won't be as famous at a well-being and wellness celebration as it would be a state band show.

2. Business Districts

If you'd prefer to grow consistently after breakfast and lunch, hit the business and monetary regions in your general vicinity. Hungry workers searching for a snappy, however delicious feast in the middle of gatherings could make some high income for you.

Park in a similar zone simultaneously consistently, and you will become acquainted with your clients by name and build up a dependable after that helps develop your business. Because of the prominence of business locale, you should hope to discover a great deal of finishing from other food trucks, and as such, you should make an effort not to set up close to one that is your immediate rivalry.

3. Ranchers Markets

Throughout the spring and mid-year months, many individuals shop at ranchers' markets to get new foods grown from the ground. This may be an excellent area to leave your food truck for at some point if you fundamentally utilize nearby sourced, natural fixings in your menu. Notwithstanding picking up new clients, you may frame new associations with nearby cultivators also.

4. Road Parking

You should have a piece of decent information on where hungry individuals are. For example, on the off chance that you have neighborhood parks in your general vicinity or chronicled destinations, many individuals rush as well. Look at the neighborhood statutes for stopping on the road close by.

If there are no lawful limitations, these could be prime spots for getting passersby's. On the off chance that there is hefty development in a specific area, you could likewise stop for some time during breakfast and lunch hours to take care of the multitude of hungry laborers.

5. School Campuses

A ton of students have discovered that the food served in their feasting lobbies to be not exactly good. Undergrads are continually moving and continually searching for fast suppers to snatch in the middle of their classes and exercises.

What's more, if it is all the same to you working late into the night, you can profit by the late-night desires that consistently hit undergrads, whether it is in the wake of a difficult evening concentrating in the school library or after a night of celebrating.

6. Truck Parks

Lately, food trucks have expanded in notoriety. To additional expand their prevalence and boost benefit, a ton of food truck proprietors have begun to cooperate for the benefit of everyone. This has offered to ascend to different food trucks leaving in an isolated area on a concurred day and time. Typically, a gathering of food trucks together in one spot can arouse individuals' curiosity more than one single truck in a specific spot.

One of the advantages of systems administration with different proprietors is that you'll get mindful of these truck leaves' area and season. It would be best if you weren't closest companions with everybody, except attempt to keep an expert connection with your "rivals" to guarantee you get welcome to these rewarding occasions.

7. Shopping Districts

Truly, most huge indoor shopping centers will have many eateries, and generally, a food court inside more modest strip shopping centers, or more modest shopping locale inside active metropolitan regions. Then again, as a rule, don't have a ton of snappy, great eats choices. These could be a decent spot to settle in at night or at the end of the week.

8. Bars and Nightclubs

If it is all the same to you working late hours, bars and dance clubs may be decent outskirts to investigate. When people drink, there is consistently the propensity they will get eager and wouldn't fret purchasing food. On the off chance that there's a mainstream bar in your general vicinity, you could wind up raking in some serious cash for only a couple of long stretches of work.

The best methodology is probably to locate the truck inside the passageway's vision (and smell sight). Along these lines, bar supporters will smell the delightful passage when entering and particularly leaving the structure. It's a triumphant recipe for a fruitful area.

Find a bar or club that ends up being reliably productive. You should make an honest effort to be on acceptable terms with the proprietor or supervisor of the spot as this kind of relationship can return a ton of benefit for you in years to come.

9. Corner Stores

With the correct methodology, service stations can end up being a great area to leave your food truck. Often, laborers in construction, delivery, or law enforcement wind up buying a 5-hour old sausage or microwaveable sandwich from a corner shop for lunch while topping off with gas. In any case, if these people can locate a superior option, they wouldn't fret putting in a couple of additional dollars to have a good dinner.

As a rule, corner store proprietors and administrators like the presence of food trucks around their premises since food trucks can cause more to notice their business and keep people in the region longer. As long as you get endorsement earlier from the business before appearing, this can be a mutually advantageous situation both for yourself and the service station.

While distinguishing great service stations to prospect, consider bigger general stores or "super" stations that get a ton of clients.

158

One spot to start the inquiry is close to significant thruways and interstates since you can wind up serving hungry voyagers.

All in all, food trucks have been ascending in prevalence throughout the long term. If you are now in the business or might want to get into the business, you need to acknowledge how significant your area is to your prosperity.

It is similarly as significant as the nature of food that you cook because regardless of whether your food is acceptable, however, it might be parked in a badly designed spot. At that point, individuals will think that it's hard to rebound. Where you leave your truck, your monetary achievement is decided. It tends to be the distinction between seven clients and seventy. To be effective, you must be seen. That implies finding the best area for your food truck.

You may discover that finding the ideal area can include experimentation, and when you locate that ideal spot, you should monitor it enviously. You can do this by conveying an organizing vehicle in front of your truck to snatch your number one spot before another person does. Word spreads, and you need to put forth a valiant effort to remain quiet about this area.

Make a point to tell individuals where you'll be. Use your site and your web-based media stages to communicate your day by day area to help people discover you. Be innovative and check your neighborhood guidelines, and you're certain to assemble a devoted clientele rapidly.

Conclusion

Food trucks are a trendy business, and of course, the food industry is booming. Many reports have come out in the past few years, claiming that the food and beverage industry will continue to grow despite the recession, which means that it is a good time to start your own food truck business.

The restaurant market is crowded, but the food truck market is still pretty new. There are niches where you can have an advantage. However, this is all always much easier said than done.

Here we outline some of the challenges that food truck owners and aspiring entrepreneurs should be aware of:

- **No frequent hours or location.** If you're always moving and vending at different events, it can be challenging for repeat customers to find you.

- **Lack of storage space**. With a restaurant, you can keep meats, dairy, and other ingredients stored in a freezer or refrigerator. With a food truck, it's tough to store a lot of food, which can make operations more complex.

- **Overnight parking and storage.** Even though you operate a food truck, you'll still need a safe place to store the vehicle overnight. Some counties require food trucks to park overnight at a commissary or commercial kitchen.

- **Competition.** With the food truck market booming, it can be difficult to break through and generate a concept that will stand out from the masses.

- **Long hours.** A food truck can require many hours of maintenance, location scouting, cleaning, event booking, and more. For example, if there is a big event, you might want to move your operation to that area. If you're going to be a food truck success, you need to follow the news.

- **Zoning laws.** It can be difficult for food truck owners to stay up to date with zoning restrictions and local ordinances regarding where they can park their truck and how long they can remain at a single location.

- **Good reputation.** Given the newness of the food truck industry, it is hard to achieve and maintain a good reputation. Many customers are still a bit hesitant to try a different business when they are unsure of where the food comes from, no matter how much your food smells good. If your business stays closed-minded and limits its client base by refusing to accept credit cards or cash, then you will find yourself isolated. Remember, you need business diversity and stability. Offer your customers food trucks that accept cash and credit cards, and they will come back again!

- **Safe place.** You need to get your food truck to this location, and the area must be sufficient for the number of customers you expect.

161

- **Well-trained staff.** The quality of your food is determined by the staff you employ. You cannot train a staff overnight, so allow yourself plenty of time to test drive your team and find people who are both experienced and motivated.

Food trucks that fail usually get the basics wrong and don't take the time to research their business or write a business plan. Sometimes their food takes too long to make, which cuts down on profitability. Sometimes, it's just a lack of marketing and planning where they'll sell. Another issue is new vendors don't understand how much work operating a food truck will actually be. You've got to be driven to start this business.

Naturally, a lot of details to the process of getting started will be unique to your city or region. As with any business, there are a lot of tiny little details that make up getting started. But take it from me and my experience, if you take it one step at a time and remember to enjoy the ride you will achieve your goal of owning and operating a food truck business of your very own. I wish you nothing but the best in your journey!